Also by James Campbell and Rob Jones ...

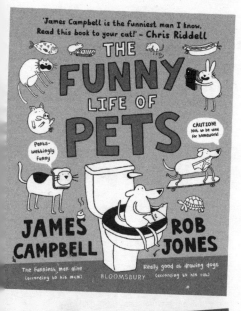

'James Campbell is the funniest man I know. Read this book to your cat!' – Chris Riddell

THE FUNNY LIFE OF PETS

CAUTION! Not to be used for homework!

Pants-wettingly funny

JAMES CAMPBELL

ROB JONES

The funniest man alive (according to his mum)

Really good at drawing dogs (according to his cat)

BLOOMSBURY

HELP!

THE FUNNY LIFE OF TEACHERS

CAUTION! Not to be used for homework!

Face-achingly funny!

JAMES CAMPBELL

ROB JONES

Will make you laugh so much snot will fly out of your nose

Really good at homework (if the homework is drawing dogs on skateboards!)

BLOOMSBURY

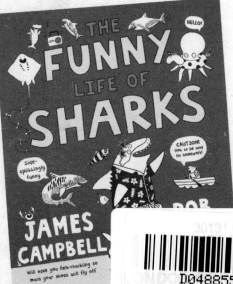

HELLO!

THE FUNNY LIFE OF SHARKS

CAUTION! Not to be used for homework!

Side-splittingly funny

JAMES CAMPBELL

Will have you fart-chuckling so much your shoes will fly off

ROB

Write YOUR OWN FUNNY Stories

Ahoy!

CAUTION! Will result in painfully funny writing!

Belly-achingly bananas

WORLD CLASS AUTHOR

ROB JONES

The man who draws with a laugh-out-loud pencil

For Hayden – who actually likes football
– James Campbell

For Jack, the biggest football fan and
Liverpool supporter I know.
– Rob Jones

BLOOMSBURY CHILDREN'S BOOKS
Bloomsbury Publishing Plc
50 Bedford Square, London, WC1B 3DP, UK
29 Earlsfort Terrace, Dublin 2, Ireland

BLOOMSBURY, BLOOMSBURY CHILDREN'S BOOKS and the Diana logo
are trademarks of Bloomsbury Publishing Plc

First published in Great Britain 2022 by Bloomsbury Publishing Plc

Text copyright © James Campbell, 2022
Illustrations copyright © Rob Jones, 2022

James Campbell and Rob Jones have asserted their rights under the Copyright, Designs
and Patents Act, 1988, to be identified as Author and Illustrator of this work

A catalogue record for this book is available from the British Library

ISBN: PB: 9781526627995 eBook: 9781526627988

2 4 6 8 10 9 7 5 3 1

Printed and bound in Great Britain by CPI (UK) Ltd, Croydon CRO 4YY

MIX
Paper from
responsible sources
FSC® C171272
FSC
www.fsc.org

To find out more about our authors and books visit www.bloomsbury.com
and sign up for our newsletters

The author and publisher recommend enabling SafeSearch when using the Internet in conjunction with
this book. We can accept no responsibility for information published on the Internet.

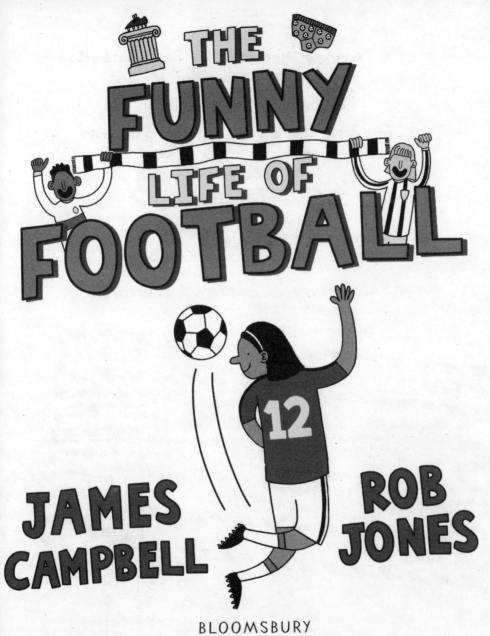

THE FUNNY LIFE OF FOOTBALL

JAMES CAMPBELL ROB JONES

BLOOMSBURY
CHILDREN'S BOOKS
LONDON OXFORD NEW YORK NEW DELHI SYDNEY

STOP!

Read this before you dare go any further ...

Fact ⚠ WARNING ⚠ WARNING ⚠ Fact

Fact Alert

Anything you think you might learn from this book might not be very accurate so should not be used in a school project or as part of your homework. And if you're ever in a quiz situation about football it's probably a bad idea to use answers found in this book. Unless you really like being wrong and getting ZERO in tests.

Fact Alert

WARNING ⚠ WARNING ⚠ Fact

Yay! I got a round one!

4

WHAT SORT OF BOOK IS THIS?

This is not a fact book as such. You won't find much practical information in here.

If you're looking for **proper** statistics and stuff about football then immediately put this book on the penalty spot and **kick it so hard** that it flies over the crossbar and you have to spend the rest of the year hiding from your fans and apologising on social media.

If it's sensible and accurate information you really want, I can recommend the following books:

I Nearly Scored Once (My Life as a Centre Half)

Sandy Bumcrack

The Incredibly Boring Life of Football.

By Anil Nildrawer

The Factual Football Encyclopaedia

by A. Ball

This book is for four types of people:

1. People who really like **playing** football. You've got a football top with your name on the back. You own more than one pair of shin pads and **you know how to do a Rainbow Flick with a grapefruit.**

2. People who love **watching** football but never actually play. You are perfectly happy on the sofa watching football, **occasionally** sitting forward if there's a free kick. You like being in a stadium, eating terrible pies and singing songs and saying 'Ooooooh' along with everyone else.

Your Name

12

My wife!

3. People who really **hate** football. You **can't think of anything worse** than running around a muddy field chasing a bouncy round thing while people cheer and yell rude words at you. Or worse, **watching other people** play football when you could be doing something useful like learn to play the piano with your nose. This book will help you look at football in a new way.

4. People who have no **interest whatsoever in football.** You've never played it, watched it, thought about it. Maybe you've **never even heard of it.** But you like **laughing** and **giggling** so much that you'll suffer an attack of fart-chuckling and release so much bum-gas that your cat will go cross-eyed and fall over.

Not normal

This is **not a normal book.** You can read it in **any order you like.** You haven't even got to the beginning yet! This book is full of **signposts** which send you to other pages. If you see something you like the look of, follow the signpost and see where it takes you.

Read a couple of random pages. **Read the book backwards.** Forwards. Sideways.

Take the book to the park, **hang upside down** from a goalpost and read it like that.

Actually, don't do that. All the blood will rush to your head and you'll look like a radish.

Which could be cool.

Warning about facts and statistics

Occasionally, this book will give you some **actual facts and statistics.**

For example, the footballer who has scored the **most** goals in a single World Cup was a French player called Just Fontaine. In 1960, he scored thirteen goals in one tournament.

But, in a few years' time will this still be the record, or will someone else have scored more goals in World Cups that **haven't happened** yet?

You have to be **careful** with facts. Facts change all the time. By the time your own children read this book, half of the facts will be **wrong.** However, all of the fictional things will still be true until the universe cracks and the centre spot at Wembley Stadium splits open to reveal a portal to another dimension!

Beginning page

Congratulations on making it to the beginning of the book. Not everyone makes it this far. Some people just read the first one or two pages and then get so hungry that they accidentally eat the book without thinking about it.

Do not eat books!

People are always saying that books are good for you, but they do not mean **in your tummy.**

For a start, you'd get indigestion and spend the whole day **farting** words!

Pardon me for being rude, it was not me, it was the 240 pages of nonsense that I ate this morning by accident.

antelope

Corner

wallaby

stadium

Then the following day you would probably **poo an alphabet!**

Do not eat books! (Please.)

You'd have to wipe your bum with an eraser!

Anyway. This is the beginning of the book. Choose a signpost of something you're interested in and turn to that page.

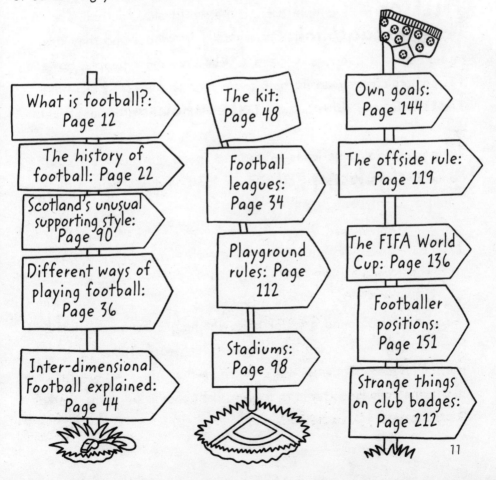

What is football?: Page 12

The history of football: Page 22

Scotland's unusual supporting style: Page 90

Different ways of playing football: Page 36

Inter-dimensional Football explained: Page 44

The kit: Page 48

Football leagues: Page 34

Playground rules: Page 112

Stadiums: Page 98

Own goals: Page 144

The offside rule: Page 119

The FIFA World Cup: Page 136

Footballer positions: Page 151

Strange things on club badges: Page 212

What is football?

Football is usually played with a ball but can be played using an empty fizzy drink can, a tennis ball, an inflated pig's bladder or two fruit bowls stuck together with strawberry jam.

Millions of people around the world play football. For some it's their **actual job.** Others do it at school and they are forced to do it because it is the **law.** For most people, however, it is something they do in their spare time to **keep fit,** have **fun** and have something to **talk about** with their friends.

One of my relatives loves football so much that he doesn't talk about **anything else.** If football didn't exist, I think he would probably be completely silent.

Maybe monks who have taken a vow of silence are just seriously into football but have never heard of it.

You can also spend a lot of time watching other people play football. On the TV or in real life. Lots of people follow a particular team. Sometimes it's the team that plays where they live and sometimes it's a team that is on the other side of the world.

Or even on a **different planet!** (The Jupiter Inter-Moon League is particularly well supported by people from the East Midlands for some reason).

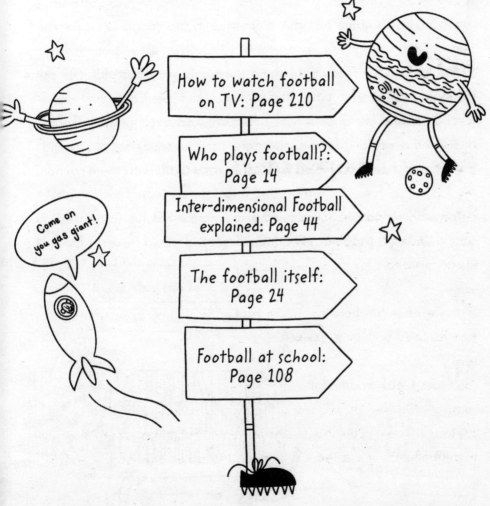

How to watch football on TV: Page 210

Who plays football?: Page 14

Inter-dimensional Football explained: Page 44

The football itself: Page 24

Football at school: Page 108

Come on you gas giant!

Who plays football?

Pretty much anyone can play football, apart from tiny babies.

I suppose you could just put a football in the middle of a parent-and-baby group at the library and watch them all roll around **not** kicking the ball. Until some annoying grown-up actually puts the ball in front of a baby and makes it kick like some sort of vomitty puppet, but this would probably turn into the most boring thing in the world after approximately five seconds so you would have to yell **'Bumpackets!'** across the library. And then the lady who runs the parent-and-baby group would tut really loudly, all the parents would stare at you like you've just licked the door handle in a doctor's waiting room and you'd have to leave the library forever.

That's what happened to me.

When I was a librarian.

No Football 🚫
or shouting bumpackets

Bumpackets

The Most Boring Thing In The World Paradox: Page 214

Most people start playing football properly when they are about five or six. At this age you can try to kick the ball towards a goal, accidentally stand on top of the ball and fall on your bottom really quickly. These are some of the **first skills** you will need.

Shooting:
Page 160

Dribbling:
Page 166

Passing:
Page 162

As you get bigger, you will learn to kick the ball properly, dribble, shoot and walk around the field yelling at your friends. You will yell things like:

Pass it!

I'm over here!

Stop hogging the ball!

I need the ball back so I can go home and eat my tea!

And then when you do get the ball, you will **hog it** and **refuse to pass** it to anyone until it's time to go home and have your tea.

If you get good at football you might play in a team of some sort. **Or** you may discover that you are **rubbish** at playing football and decide simply to watch other people play and shout at them. You'll probably shout things like:

Football match food: Page 111

Playground rules: Page 112

How to watch football on TV: Page 210

Different ways of playing football: Page 36

Please hurry up and score! I need to go home and have my tea.

Football is also a big part of para sports. There's wheelchair football, football for people who are blind or visually impaired and football for people with many different disabilities.

There's even a type of football for older and less mobile people called Walking Football.

As far as I can tell though, there is no football for **bananas.** Bananas are not allowed to play football. Maybe that's why they are so angry.

Where is football played?

Professional football happens on something called a **pitch.**

Ideally, the pitch should be flat, but some are famously slightly sloped, which means you're either playing uphill or downhill.

Many school football pitches are **ridiculously** sloped. Particularly in the Highlands of Scotland where some are on the side of a mountain and goalkeepers have to be **tied to a rock** to stop them from rolling into the sea.

In the park, however, the pitch can be any size. I particularly like it when a pitch has no edges and you can go as wide as you like without the ball ever being out of play until it goes into a river or someone else's picnic.

One of the great things about football is that you don't even need a field to play on. It doesn't even have to be grass. A bit of concrete or an alleyway is fine.

I can remember spending hours with friends kicking the ball at a really **big wall.** It was so much fun and the wall never complained.

League table of picnic ruinations: Page 222

The beginning of my footballing career: Page 30

Stadiums: Page 98

The Great Stamford Meadows Match: Page 216

Subbuteo: Page 58

Table football: Page 60

Inter-dimensional Football explained: Page 44

Using football as a way to communicate better

The **best thing** about kicking a ball about with your friends is that you **don't have to talk to each other.** The ball becomes the focus. Doing this you can build close friendships without ever having a conversation about anything more important than how well you each kicked the ball.

You could possibly mix things up a bit by yelling out **emotional questions** whilst playing football.

> Nice save mate.

> I know I'm a bit old for it, but I still cuddle my teddies all night long. What about you?

Or, if you want to have a **difficult conversation** with someone you can have a kick about in the garden whilst you're doing it.

You don't really look at each other. You look at the ball.

It's similar with watching football together. You could probably drop in all sorts of things whilst watching a really good match.

I'll go in goal. You take penalties at me. And while you're doing it I'll tell you how I'm secretly in love with your sister.

Dad, I have failed all of my subjects at school and the head teacher has asked me to leave and go to a school on the moon.

Don't worry son. We're 3-0 up.

How to watch football on TV: Page 210

Penalties: Page 170

The Great Stamford Meadows Match: Page 216

How to tell the universe what you want: Page 186

The history of football

The first recorded history of people playing with a ball dates back **3,000 years,** when the Meso-American peoples played a game involving a ball of **stone.** Historians think that the ball represented the Sun, and at the end of the game the losing players would be **sacrificed** to the gods!

Which is a bit extreme.

And why are you here so young?

I missed a penalty.

The first written records of people playing the game of football start around the 12th century CE. And through the Middle Ages people would play a kind of **mob football** which was very rough, involved picking the ball up if you wanted to and could last all day. It seems any number of people could play in the same match and the only definite rule was that you weren't allowed to **murder** anyone!

That is still a rule today.

Rules you didn't know existed: Page 117

Playground rules: Page 112

Japanese keepy-uppy

In ancient Japan, a game was played called Kemari. Six or seven people would stand in a circle and kick a ball backwards and forwards, seeing **how long** they could keep the ball from touching the ground.

Keepy-uppy, of course, is a great way to improve your skills, especially if you don't have anyone to play actual football with. Or even if you're just waiting for something to start.

PARENT: What are you doing?

CHILD: Keepy-uppies. I'm just waiting for the comedy show to start.

PARENT: It has started.

CHILD: No it hasn't. That's just a man talking.

ME: Ermmm ...

Ball control: Page 158

Passing: Page 162

Dribbling: Page 166

Free kicks: Page 177

The football itself

Footballs used to be made of a pig's **bladder!**

The bladder is the bit that holds all the **wee-wee.** So that means in those day pigs must have been going around not being able to have a wee-wee. And all because of football!

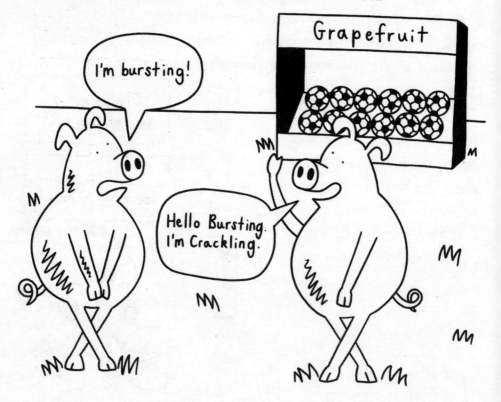

Bladders were used because they are **round.** Most materials are flat. It's very **difficult** to make something round from something flat. Today, footballs are either leather or plastic and are made from **12** pentagons and **20** hexagons, all stitched together. When the ball is filled with air, the centres of all of those shapes bulge, making the whole thing spherical.

However, all sorts of things can be used instead of a ball. As a child, the footballing legend Pelé often used a grapefruit. To me that seems like a waste of a **grapefruit,** but my mum hates grapefruit and says that using them as footballs is the best thing you can do with the horrible things.

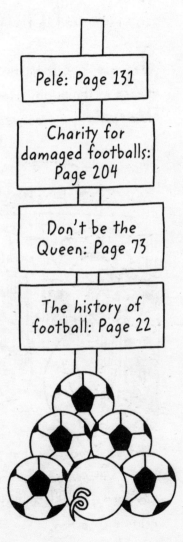

Pelé: Page 131

Charity for damaged footballs: Page 204

Don't be the Queen: Page 73

The history of football: Page 22

Kings who tried to ban football

Because mob football was so **violent,** many kings and queens of England tried to ban it. Imagine trying to make football **illegal!**

Edward III and Edward IV both tried to stop people playing because it **distracted** them from learning how to use a bow and arrow.

Shane! Stop playing with that pig's bladder! Come inside and do your archery homework!

Richard II and Henry IV also tried to ban football for similar reasons.

In the 16th century, Henry VIII made a law to stop football because it was causing too many **fights.** The thing is though, Henry VIII owned the first pair of football boots that anyone has ever heard of. So maybe he liked to play football **secretly,** inside his castles.

Often rulers will make **two sets** of rules - one for all of us, and one for themselves. I can't prove it, but I reckon that during the time Henry VIII made football illegal he would **sneak** up to a castle near Durham to have secret matches with his family.

Why are people still using Roman numerals?: Page 70

The history of football: Page 22

The history of the kit: Page 50

Penalties: Page 170

Footballer positions: Page 151

The beginning of the FA: Page 28

Henry VIII was famously **horrible.** He had six wives. He had two of them **executed!** He also completely **dismantled** the church! He **dissolved** monasteries! And somehow found time to ban football. What a strange man!

Fortunately, the ban didn't last long and Henry's successor - the young Edward VI - went on to play centre-half for Bolton Wanderers.

The beginning of the FA

The Football Association (FA) was founded in 1863 in order to establish a series of **rules** that everyone could follow. Before this, football was only played in certain private schools. Each school had its own version so when teams tried to play against each other they found they were all playing different rules!

The rules that the FA came up with included:

The match should be 90 minutes long (which is a long time if it's **cold and rainy**).

All players should be able to ride a giant bicycle.

The ball should be a particular size and weight.

Players are **not allowed** to kick each other in the shins!

Are you sure that's a regulation FA-sized ball?

If you ever find yourself losing a game, it's perfectly acceptable to **change the rules** and make up your own version. When I was five, I decided to distract the opposition by only wearing my pants. Everyone complained and my auntie fainted, so I tried to start my own game of Pants Football but no one else wanted to join in. Sometimes I still play **Pants Football** but I still haven't managed to find any teammates, so mainly it is just me, on my own, running around the garden in my pants trying to bend the ball around the damson tree.

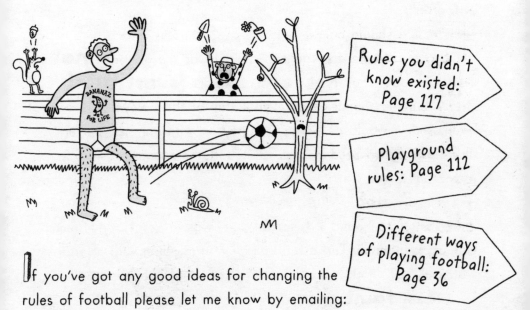

Rules you didn't know existed: Page 117

Playground rules: Page 112

Different ways of playing football: Page 36

If you've got any good ideas for changing the rules of football please let me know by emailing: pleasestopsendingmeemails@whatever.com

The beginning of my footballing career

Anyone for football?

I have a confession to make.

The truth is that when I was at primary school, I was **rubbish** at football.

There were twelve boys in our class. I was the only one **not** in the football team. **Not even as a substitute!** The PE teacher decided that even if one of their players were to be injured, it would be better to carry on with only ten players than have me involved in any way. That's how disastrously bad at football I was.

Even out of school, I was terrible. If I was in a park and some kids accidentally kicked a football over in my direction, often they would all yell, 'Kick it back, mate!'. When that happened ... I would just **faint.**

Or pretend to faint.

On the **rare** occasions when I did try and kick the ball back, I would usually loop it over my head and end up kicking it in the other direction!

So, I would have to pick the ball up and **carry** it to them!

Somebody once suggested that maybe if I tried to deliberately kick the ball in the opposite direction, then it might go towards the people who wanted their ball back.

The next time this happened, I tried it. A ball rolled over to me in the park, and everyone shouted, 'Kick it back!'. So, I placed myself between them and the ball and attempted to kick it away from them. Somehow, however, I **suddenly** developed the skills of Lionel Messi and kicked the ball so hard and fast that it curved around two trees and then dropped into a bin. I was really pleased with myself until I saw all the footballing people running towards me with very **angry faces.**

Lionel Messi: Page 114

Passing: Page 162

Free kicks: Page 177

Corners: Page 180

Football at school: Page 108

My footballing career continues!: Page 42

Football leagues

Handball!

Professional football is **divided** up into leagues. Some of them are played on land, but 20,000 of these leagues are actually **under the sea!** The most popular one being the **Mermaid Super-Trident League.**

Most sea creatures play some sort of football. **Sharks** make very good centre-forwards as no one wants to tackle them and **rays** play on the wing. **Octopuses**, however, have been banned from playing football as no one can tell which of their tentacles is a leg and which of their tentacles is an arm so referees can't call handball.*

But anyway, on the land and for humans, each country has different leagues for different **qualities** of teams. In the UK, the **top league** is the Premiership for men and the FA Women's Super League for women. Whereas in Italy it's Serie A (one for men, one for women), in Spain it's Primera Division de La Liga (one for men, one for women) and in Germany it's the Bundesliga for men, and the Frauen Bundesliga for women!

*Fun fact: octopuses don't actually have tentacles, as all of their limbs are called arms. So it's ALWAYS a handball!

Promotion and relegation

After each season, football teams can get promoted to the league **above,** or relegated (demoted) to the one **below.**

Getting promoted is a **big deal.** It means bigger matches, better opponents and more people buying tickets. This means more money to spend on better players.

Getting relegated is very **embarrassing** and means a team will have to survive for at least a year with smaller crowds and less money.

If your team gets relegated you won't be able to wear your team's football shirt for the rest of the summer unless it's inside out.

If your team gets promoted, the following September you are legally allowed to wear your football top on your first day back at school. Unless you live in one of the following countries:
England, Scotland, Wales, Northern Ireland, Republic of Ireland,
France, Spain, Germany, Belgium, Netherlands, Poland, Austria, Czech Republic ...
Bangladesh, Myanmar, China, Singapore ... USA, Australia, New Zealand, Japan ... etc. etc.

Different ways of playing football

There are many different ways to play football. It depends who or where you are and how many people you've got to play with.

FA rules say football must be played with **11 people** on each side. One of them must be the goalkeeper and there must be **two goals** at either end of the pitch.

FIVE-A-SIDE rules allow for smaller teams on **smaller** pitches and with smaller goals. Only the goalkeeper can enter the goal area, and play doesn't stop for substitutions.

STREET FOOTBALL doesn't have any rules – but there are **traditions.** Matches can last for a whole day but will break for dinnertime when you will go home, eat as quickly as possible and then get back to the game. Jumpers, coats or even younger brothers and sisters can be used as goalposts. **There are no referees.** Anyone kicking the ball over a fence must get it back, even if there are dogs involved or an angry vicar.

BLIND FOOTBALL is played on a five-a-side pitch. Each team has four blind players and a sighted goalkeeper. The ball contains metal shards which rattle around as the ball moves.

POWERCHAIR (WHEELCHAIR) FOOTBALL is for people who are users of either manual wheelchairs (that you use your hands to move around with) or powerchairs which are electric ones. The chairs are modified with bumpers put across the front. This is what players use to hit the ball with.

WALKING FOOTBALL is great for **older footballers** and people who are less mobile or get tired more easily. Running is not allowed, nor is jogging, meaning if you're in goal and the ball is on the other end of the pitch, there's always time to squeeze in a quick nap before the next attack.

BACK GARDEN FOOTBALL can be very **complicated.** The pitch may be rectangular but is more likely to be oddly shaped. Sometimes there is a tree in the middle. There is usually only one goal and one goalkeeper. Rules are particular to the garden but might include:

- Do not hit the greenhouse.

- Do not damage any flowers.

- Do not tackle toddlers.

- Allow toddlers to score goals even though they don't know how to fart without pooing themselves let alone take a free kick.

- Dogs can use all four of their feet and their nose but not their teeth.

- Don't shout too much – Nan is trying to sleep.

INTER-DIMENSIONAL FOOTBALL is like 11-a-side but has extra rules to accommodate various **timelines, multiple universes** and different **galaxies.** My favourite rule is that no one player can compete in more than one incarnation in the same game. This is to stop players from going back in time and making up teams consisting only of themselves. The thing with Inter-dimensional Football is that the more closely you examine the rules, the less clear they become. The only way to play it perfectly is to **not pay any attention** to the rules at all.

The history of the kit: Page 50

Football leagues: Page 34

The kit: Page 48

Football at school: Page 108

The beginning of the FA: Page 28

Gary Lineker pooed himself

World's Most Public Poo

Probably the **most extraordinary** thing that has happened on a football pitch was in the 1990 World Cup in Italy.

Gary Lineker was England's captain and top **Fox in the Box.**

International idioms: Page 205

In their first group match, though, he was also their **Rumbly in the Tumbly** because he had an **upset stomach.**

At one point, Lineker lunged for the ball and as he did so felt everything give way in his bottom department and realised with horror that he had **accidentally pooed himself.**

Now, I don't know when the last time you pooed yourself was, but I'm guessing it was not in front of **33,000 people** with another **100 million** or so watching on the TV.

How to watch football on TV: Page 210

That's right. Gary Lineker became the world record holder for the world's most public poo.

He did his best to carry on but says he found it difficult to run properly with poo slopping about in his shorts. There was, however, one **advantage.** Strikers often find themselves closely marked by defenders, but after pooing himself Lineker found he always had plenty of space around him.

Footballer positions: Page 151

Marking: Page 174

England went on to the semi-finals that year where they were cruelly beaten by Germany on penalties. But Gary Lineker proved you could still play well, even with poo in your pants. He went on to invent a pair of **poo-proof pants** for anyone feeling they might be in a similar situation. I'm so excited about writing this book that I'm wearing my pair **NOW!**

The kit: Page 48

The history of the kit: Page 50

The FIFA World Cup: Page 136

My footballing career continues!

My son, Hayden, was five when I first met him, and he was already really keen on football. Hayden had been to **actual matches** and everything!

His best football story was when his teammate scored an **own goal** – Hayden didn't realise that this was a bad thing and celebrated along with the opposition.

Own goals:
Page 144

Goal celebrations:
Page 142

I found that I was unexpectedly **brilliant** at kicking a football around in the back garden with him. We set up a goal using garden chairs as posts and the fence as the net. And then we would take turns to fire penalties at each other.

There was a wheat field on the other side of the fence and if you **skied** the ball you would have to go and get it back. We must have spent hours looking for that ball, probably covering ourselves in pesticides and other poisons. I don't think Hayden suffered any long-lasting effects. Although since then he does scream in the middle of the night and smells like **raspberries.** And one of his ears fell off.

Different ways of playing football:
Page 36

Penalties:
Page 170

Anyway. At this point in my life, I hadn't really kicked a football for about twenty years. But I was amazed at how quickly it all came back to me. It was like my legs and feet had remembered how to play even if my head hadn't. After a while there was no doubt about it:

I needed to tell the universe!

I was better than a five-year-old at football!

International idioms:
Page 205

43

Inter-dimensional Football explained

The key to Inter-dimensional Football is to use the **wonderful weirdness** of the universe as a tool for playing football.

For example, according to the normal laws of physics, if you were to kick a football with a certain amount of force towards a goal, scientists could **predict** exactly how it would rise and fall.

So we can see whether the ball will dip enough to score a goal at the other end.

BUT, those laws of physics don't actually work with things that are incredibly BIG (like planets) or incredibly SMALL (like subatomic particles, which are the **tiniest** things known to science).

If a football behaved like a subatomic particle and you took a free kick, the ball might travel like this ...

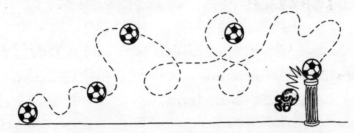

... And then just before it got to the goal, it might just disappear and not exist anymore. Or there might be two of them. And one of them would be French.

So if anything is possible in the universe, surely anything is possible in football? **That's where Inter-dimensional Football comes in.**

Why not imagine yourself in a possible universe in which you are a professional footballer. And you play for your favourite club or even for an entirely imaginary team made up of all your footballing heroes.

You can **bend the ball**, make it **wiggle** through the air, or even make it **disappear!**

Imagine yourself as your favourite player, scoring a ridiculous goal with ridiculous **space-bending skills.**

This is Inter-dimensional Football. There are no limits to what you can **do** with your mind.

I have formed a team called Stewmarket Inter-dimensional Wanderers. We play different **planets** and **galaxies.** We also play backwards and forwards in time. Players slip in and out in quite an informal way, but regular players include Lionel Messi, Gary Lineker and Gandalf from *Lord of the Rings.*

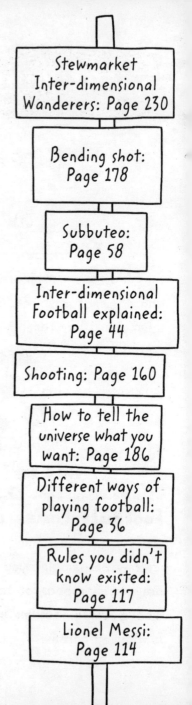

Stewmarket Inter-dimensional Wanderers: Page 230

Bending shot: Page 178

Subbuteo: Page 58

Inter-dimensional Football explained: Page 44

Shooting: Page 160

How to tell the universe what you want: Page 186

Different ways of playing football: Page 36

Rules you didn't know existed: Page 117

Lionel Messi: Page 114

GRAEME SOUNESS

FOOTBALLING ERA:
1970s, 1980s and 1990s.

DESCRIPTION:
Person from the 1980s.

PLAYED FOR:
Liverpool, Glasgow
Rangers, Scotland
and more.

POSITION: Midfielder.

Famous for: Being a very physical player. Souness was a player-manager at Glasgow Rangers which means you have to shout at yourself a lot, tell yourself what to do and complain about yourself to other people.

The manager:
Page 189

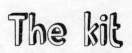 # The kit

If you want to play football in a **serious** way you will need certain items of equipment.

If you want to play football in a **silly** way you will need a bath full of jelly, a wallaby costume and a photo of your chosen grown-up (I've chosen my mum).

For most team games you will need a shirt, shorts, socks, shin pads, football boots, underwear, nipple protectors, a moustache and a woolly hat if it's cold.

Probably the most iconic part of a footballer's kit is the shirt. But boots and shin pads are also important. If you toe-punt the ball with bare feet, you will roll around on the floor holding your toe, looking like a **soggy pretzel** for at least five minutes.

And careful with shin pads – they have a habit of working their way around the back of your leg. This makes you walk like a **robot** and you'll find it very difficult to score any goals except backwards.

If you are the goalkeeper you will need a different coloured shirt from everyone else and a pair of gloves. You're allowed to borrow someone's work gloves if you've nothing else.

Lev Yashin, who was Russia's best goalkeeper of all time, used his Auntie Jenny's **gardening gloves** for most international matches.

Lev Yashin:
Page 86

The history
of the kit:
Page 50

Footballer
positions:
Page 151

Goalkeeper
training:
Page 176

The history of the kit

Professional football teams have always worn **identical shirts** so that everyone knows who is on which team. In the 19th century, goalkeepers wore the same shirt as their teammates, but in 1909 they were given permission to wear a different colour.

Before the 1890s, footballers wore long trousers but then switched to long shorts which they called **'knickerbockers'**, or 'knickers' for short.

In 1900, Charlie Roberts, who played for Manchester United, decided to be **daring** and wore a pair of short knickers to play football.

Stadiums: Old Trafford: Page 100

Eventually, all footballers wore short knickerbockers which they called 'shorts', which were short shorts but not as short as Charlie Roberts' knickers. Short short shorts were not worn again until the 1980s. Thankfully they are now illegal in most civilised countries.

The first recorded pair of football boots were bought by Henry VIII in 1536.

Kings who tried to ban football: Page 26

Before shin pads were invented, Victorian footballers used to tuck a **badger** into

each of their socks to absorb the impact of any wayward tackles.

The kit: Page 48

Gary Lineker pooed himself: Page 40

Over the centuries, footballers have worn all sorts of different **underwear.** Lionel Messi wears frilly **knickers.** Cristiano Ronaldo wears **special boxers** made of gold. Mia Hamm wore her **rainbow Barbie** ones. After 1990, Gary Lineker always wore his special **poo-proof pants** which have strongly elasticated legs, allowing him to poo himself during every match without anyone noticing.

MATTHIAS SINDELAR

FOOTBALLING ERA:
1920s and 1930s.

DESCRIPTION:
So lightly built he
was known as
The Paper Man.

PLAYED FOR:
Austria.

POSITION: Forward.

Famous for: Being a footballer who **stood up to Hitler!** In 1938, when Austria played against Germany, the Nazis (who ruled Germany) had told the Austrians not to score any goals. The Nazis had also taken control of Austria and it was important to their leader, Adolf Hitler, that Germany was seen to be unbeatable in every way. Sindelar did as he was told for almost the whole match, but right at the end popped in two **brilliant goals** and then celebrated wildly right in front of all the Nazi officials.

Computer football

It is now possible to be completely brilliant at football by using only your **thumbs!**

Most children have some sort of **time limit** when it comes to computer games. Here are some of the restrictions that you might have:

- **One Hour:** That's it. Just 60 minutes and then you have to switch it off.

- **Not On School Nights:** You'll need a good night's sleep before your test.

- **Just 30 Minutes And Then You Must Have An Apple:** (We don't talk to those people.)

- **No Computer Games At All:** You live in a yurt and your parents macramé their own yoghurt.

I think it really depends on what your parents or guardians are doing. If they are in the kitchen with some friends ... having a party ... you can play computer games for as long as you like.

I haven't been to the toilet for 13 hours. Who cares? I just use my special Gary Lineker Pants.

You are disgusting. But you are brilliant at playing football.

If you don't have anyone to play against you can always play against the computer. As you get better you can make it harder for yourself. Or you can just leave it in **easy-mode** and win every match 12-0.

I can't believe you've scored 13 hat tricks in this game.

I know. I'm playing against the washing machine.

Or you could always train your dog to play computer games against you. I'll warn you though. They do **cheat.**

What are you talking about? It was the paw of God!

Personally, I think it's much better to kick a ball around outside. I never play computer games. Not because I don't like them. Unfortunately, I like them so much I can't play them any more.

When you're a child there is usually someone to tell you to **switch the computer off** and go to bed. But when you're a grown-up, there is no one to tell you this. For me the whole thing got out of hand until eventually I realised that I was playing far too much. So I had to stop completely.

I'm not saying that computer games are bad. **BUT,** since I gave up I have published ten books and am now an international bestselling author. And my thumbs have fallen off.

How to tell the universe what you want: Page 186

Hand of God: Page 66

Handball: Page 130

The FIFA World Cup: Page 136

Gary Lineker pooed himself: Page 40

Penalties: Page 170

DIEGO MARADONA

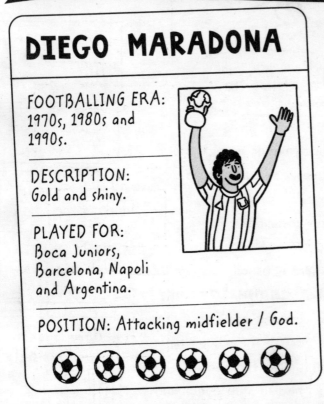

FOOTBALLING ERA: 1970s, 1980s and 1990s.

DESCRIPTION: Gold and shiny.

PLAYED FOR: Boca Juniors, Barcelona, Napoli and Argentina.

POSITION: Attacking midfielder / God.

Famous for: A seemingly **magical** ability to dribble the ball and outwit defenders. Being short, Maradona had a low centre of gravity which allowed him to pivot and spin, sending defenders **flying** in all directions. Aged sixteen he made his international debut for Argentina, and then dominated professional football during the 1980s. He was nicknamed the Golden Boy by some, and simply God by others.

In the 1986 World Cup against England, Maradona scored twice. His second goal is reckoned by most people to be the greatest goal of the 20th century, but the first was extremely controversial. So controversial in fact that it is known as the Hand of God incident and gets its own page!

Brilliant stat: Maradona may have been the **most gifted footballer of all time.** During his career, he scored 259 goals in 491 matches.

Hand of God:
Page 66

Stadiums:
Estadio Azteca:
Page 102

Handball:
Page 130

The FIFA
World Cup:
Page 136

Golden balls

Hand of God

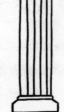

Subbuteo

When I was a child, everyone had a Subbuteo set. You had all these little plastic player-pieces to flick around on a felt football pitch and try and hit the ball with.

Unfortunately, no one really wanted to play with me so I'd spend hours just trying to flick players at the ball for no real reason.

This is how **Inter-dimensional Football** first began. I imagined the pieces were all my different footballing **heroes.** These pieces also had a habit of getting trodden on, chewed by the dog or eaten by my nan. So, after a while I started using other sorts of toys as footballers.

I still remember the day when Luke Skywalker and Lego zookeeper joined the red team.

Being five times as big as everyone else, the young Jedi made a great Number 9. The Lego man was less successful as it couldn't properly open its legs so kicking the ball was a little difficult. In the second half, the blue team brought on a giant Kermit the Frog puppet who just laid across the whole goal making it impossible for anyone to score until Luke Skywalker used the force to lift the massive frog and drop it back in the swamp from which it came.

Inter-dimensional Football explained: Page 44

Shooting: Page 160

Who should be your footballing hero?: Page 84

Tactics: Park the bus: Page 196

Stewmarket Inter-dimensional Wanderers: Page 230

Footballer positions: Page 151

Table football

This is a brilliant invention. The footballers are held by **twizzly sticks** that you use to hit the ball into the opposite goal.

You are not allowed to spin them. Spinning is **against the rules** and if anyone does spin them you must shout, 'Oy! No spinnies!'

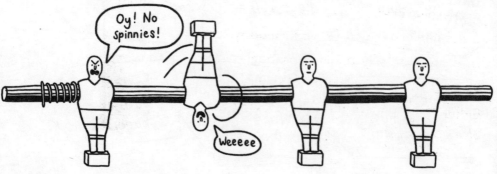

The thing is though, spinning them is a lot of fun and can accidentally cause the ball to travel at such speed that it flies across the room and lands in someone's fizzy drink!

Spinnies are also illegal in real football because they make players get dizzy and fall over. Having said that, **Bicycle Kicks** do happen quite a lot. That's when a player leaps into the air and spins around upside down, then kicks the ball over their head and towards the goal.

If this works, it looks **brilliant.** If it doesn't, you look **really silly** and everyone laughs at you. There is also a danger of landing on your head which is worse than silly and will probably end up with you leaving the match early and going to hospital in the back of someone else's Volvo.

Ridiculous goals:
Page 140

Signature moves:
Page 63

Rules you didn't know existed:
Page 117

The referee:
Page 116

EUSÉBIO

FOOTBALLING ERA:
1950s, 1960s and 1970s.

DESCRIPTION:
Strong and powerful.

PLAYED FOR:
Benfica and Portugal.

POSITION: Forward.

BONUS STUFF: He had a habit of saluting opposition goalkeepers when they saved his shots. Which is nice.

Famous for: Being probably the greatest Portuguese player of all time. Born in Mozambique, Eusébio would **sneak** out of school to play football on the streets with bare feet and a **sock stuffed with newspapers** instead of a ball. As a teenager, he was scouted by a Portuguese team and moved to Portugal where he became the first African-born footballing superstar.

Brilliant stats: Eusébio was the highest scoring player of the 1966 World Cup. Over his career he scored 733 goals in 745 matches.

Who should be your footballing hero?: Page 84

Signature moves

This is when you invent or do a particular **trick** so well that you become known for it. Professional footballers' tricks include the **Cruyff Turn, La Croqueta**, the **Flipflap**, the **Body Feint**, the **Electric Boogaloo**, the **Rainbow Flick** and the **Cristiano Chop**.

My signature move is using my face to stop the ball. I call it the Campbell Soup. No one else, however, seems to have noticed this or tried to copy me.

Hup hup!

My daughter, Daphne, has a signature move which I call the **Daphne Hup.** Whenever she's dribbling she sort of jumps around the ball saying 'Hup hup' to herself. It has no effect on the ball at all but makes it seem like she must be doing something incredibly complicated so no one tackles her.

Ridiculous goals: Page 140

You could also try copying other players' signature moves. Look up Jay-Jay Okocha's Rainbow Flick, where he puts his foot under the ball and **flicks** it up over his head. This looks really easy. When I try to do a Rainbow Flick it usually lands in one of the trees, the paddling pool or **in my own face.**

Or why not try using football moves in the rest of your life.

If you're fighting with your sister over the last chip, try a Lionel Messi Fork Feint. Just drop your shoulder one way but lunge the other way with the fork. Everyone will think you're a genius. **Or you might get ketchup thrown at you.**

Spanish footballer Andrés Iniesta famously does a move called La Croqueta where he scoops the ball from one foot to the other. A *croqueta* however, is also a type of Spanish **mashed potato.**

Why not try doing La Croqueta in the dinner hall at school with an actual ball of mashed potato ... actually ... no. That's a very silly idea. If you do that your own signature move will become known as Getting Sent to the Head Teacher and Missing Playtime for a Week.

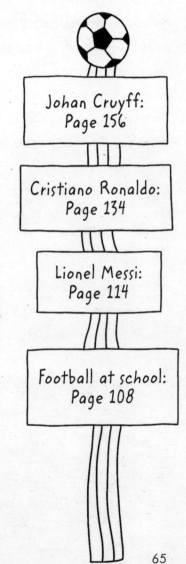

Johan Cruyff:
Page 156

Cristiano Ronaldo:
Page 134

Lionel Messi:
Page 114

Football at school:
Page 108

Hand of God

One of the **most famous things** that has ever happened on a football pitch was during the 1986 World Cup when England played Argentina.

Four years before, there had been an actual war between these countries, so this match was very much seen as a football version of the war. Argentina wanted **revenge.** Their biggest weapon was, of course, **Diego Maradona,** who was such a brilliant player he might be able to win a World Cup all on his own.

At the beginning of the second half, the ball looped into the air towards the English goalkeeper. Maradona jumped up, held his hand next to his head and then **punched** the ball into the goal!

Everyone around him called handball.

Handball:
Page 130

Diego Maradona:
Page 56

Somehow though, the referee didn't see this and gave the goal. Maradona immediately celebrated and claimed it had been the **'Hand of God'.**

In those days there was no VAR and whatever **decision** a referee made was the one you had to accept, for **good or for bad.**

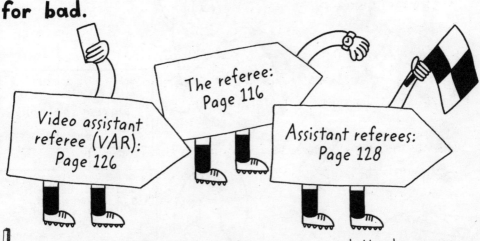

Video assistant referee (VAR): Page 126

The referee: Page 116

Assistant referees: Page 128

I had a similar incident in the garden. I was in goal. Hayden was shooting at me. I **dived** to save the ball. Just at that moment though the dog ran across the garden, jumped at the ball and knocked it in.

We call this the **Hand of Dog incident,** and even though the dog claimed the goal as her own she wasn't even supposed to be playing at the time. I said if she was playing she was on my side because I'm the one that feeds her, but Hayden said he had talked to her earlier about forming a dog-human super team that would enter the Inter-dimensional Football League and win the Multiverse Cup.

Different ways of playing football: Page 36

Inter-dimensional Football explained: Page 44

Stewmarket Inter-dimensional Wanderers: Page 230

Famous for:

Being one of the greatest goalkeepers ever. Solo has won countless matches for the USA by pulling off **outrageous** saves and stopping shots most mortal keepers wouldn't have been able to touch.

Bonus stuff:

Solo campaigns for gender equality and was part of the movement that is slowly aiming to achieve equal pay between men and women footballers.

HOPE SOLO

FOOTBALLING ERA:
2000s, 2010s.

DESCRIPTION:
Superhuman saver.

PLAYED FOR:
USA.

POSITION: Goalkeeper.

Equal pay:
Page 80

Why are people still using Roman numerals?

Apparently, it's not **enough** just to learn all of the modern numbers. You have to be able to work out how the Romans did counting too! People put Roman numerals on things like coins and after the names of kings and queens. It does make things look **more impressive.**

Henry IV looks like a name of a king.

Henry 4 looks like an app.

So what do they all mean? Well, firstly you need to know what each letter means.

$$
\begin{array}{rcl}
I &=& 1 \\
V &=& 5 \\
X &=& 10 \\
L &=& 50 \\
C &=& 100 \\
D &=& 500 \\
M &=& 1000
\end{array}
$$

When you want to say other numbers, however, things get more complicated.

III = 3

but, IV = 4 because it is one (I) before five (V). IC is one before 100 which is 99. But you could also write 99 as XCIX.

In fact, you can write most numbers in all sorts of ways with Roman numerals. They are very complicated!

In football, you might notice that when people write down the members of a team they are called the Starting XI. Not the Starting 11. This is because 'The Starting 11' might be confused as the player with the Number 11 shirt.

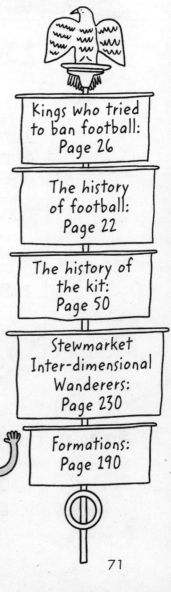

Kings who tried to ban football: Page 26

The history of football: Page 22

The history of the kit: Page 50

Stewmarket Inter-dimensional Wanderers: Page 230

Formations: Page 190

ZICO

FOOTBALLING ERA:
1970s and 1980s.

DESCRIPTION:
Legend.

PLAYED FOR:
Flamengo, Udinese
and Brazil.

POSITION: Attacking midfielder.

Famous for: His **amazing free kicks.** Zico was one of the first players to **bend the ball** in extraordinary ways. After training, he would stay behind on his own practising free kicks. People said that when Flamengo were given a direct free kick it was almost like getting a penalty. That was how likely Zico was to score.

Don't be the Queen

When I was little, older children would often play football in the street. Those football teams could be tight knit. So tight knit, in fact, that sometimes **outsiders** weren't even allowed to play. If you wanted to join in, you were usually given a silly position to trick you into thinking you weren't being **left out.** One of those roles was the Queen. To be the Queen, you had to sit on the sidelines and watch the whole match, smiling and waving continually from beginning to end.

Make sure that never happens to you. Older children, and indeed grown-ups, often give children pointless roles or send them on silly missions just to get them out of the way for a while.

Watch out for these. If you ever get sent on a pointless mission, **refuse.** And then rebel. Such a mission might involve getting one of the following items:

- Tartan paint
- Elbow grease
- A left-handed screwdriver
- A long weight

Also, watch out if you are asked to play any of the following roles:

- Any member of the royal family that just sits and watches what's going on without actually doing anything.

- A goalpost

- A football

If you are ever asked to do any of these things you must **stamp** your feet, **scream, stomp** about with pointy elbows and **INSIST** that you are allowed to be a proper part of what is going on.

One girl I know that had to be the Queen when they were little, later ended up as a really good goalkeeper. However, for some reason, whenever she was in goal she would sing **pop songs** throughout the game. I'm not sure whether this was a way of keeping focused or just a tactic to put off the other team's strikers. Either way – it's **brilliant.**

Shooting:
Page 160

Tactics:
Page 194

Footballer
positions:
Page 151

Goalkeeper
training:
Page 176

The football
itself:
Page 24

MEGAN RAPINOE

FOOTBALLING ERA:
2010s , 2020s.

DESCRIPTION:
Purple hair!

PLAYS FOR: USA.

POSITION:
Midfielder / winger.

BONUS STUFF: Rapinoe sees herself as an entertainer too. Her 122nd-minute cross in the 2019 semi-final against Brazil is one of the best goals ever!

Famous for: Becoming captain for the USA and leading them to win the Olympic Gold in 2016 and the World Cup in 2019. She also uses her position to talk about human rights. In 2016, she took the knee during the national anthem to protest against police brutality. She also campaigns for gender equality and LGBTQ+ rights.

Auntie Lisa

My sister-in-law, known as Auntie Lisa, is the **best** footballer in our whole entire family. She started playing in her garden and the playground at school, and now says she can't remember ever **not** playing football.

In the 1980s, Auntie Lisa went to a small village primary school where she was by far the **best player** on the football team. And because she was so good, no one really noticed that she was quite different from everyone else in the team in one particular way.

Football match today
kick off 3 pm
NO GIRLS ALLOWED

Auntie Lisa was a GIRL.

AUNTIE LISA
11

All was fine until the time came for their first match against another local school. Auntie Lisa turned up to play with everyone else and was wearing the same kit as everyone else, but before the game started the other team's head teacher announced that **girls were not allowed to play football.** It was against the rules. So the match went ahead without her – she wasn't even allowed to watch the game or be involved in any way.

This reminds me of a story about a team of women footballers who played in England during the First World War. At that time, lots of factories formed teams from the women workers. The most famous was Dick, Kerr Ladies F.C., who were **really** good and **really** popular. Their games did a lot to keep up morale during difficult times, but they became **so** popular that they, along with other women's teams, were **banned** from playing football by the Football Association. This ban stayed in place for fifty years and was a big setback for women's football. Perhaps if this ban had never happened, I could be writing about Auntie Lisa the famous football star. But sadly I'm not.

Thankfully women's football is now getting the recognition it deserves and I (and Auntie Lisa) can't wait to see where it goes next.

Now Auntie Lisa gets to **play** as much football as she likes, and **watch** as much football as she likes too. She gets so excited whenever women's football is on the TV that I have to wear ear muffs to **shield my ear drums** from her cheering!

When I'm playing Inter-dimensional Football I often put Auntie Lisa in as midfielder. We played the **Dirty XI** recently and she successfully kept **Voldemort** from scoring, and when the game went to penalties she was first up to face **Darth Vader.** After a couple of deep breaths she smashed the ball into the goal before the Sith Lord even had time to say, 'I have you now'.

Inter-dimensional Football explained: Page 44

Stewmarket Inter-dimensional Wanderers: Page 230

Footballer positions: Page 151

Equal Pay

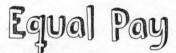

In most professions, it is the law that if two people are doing the same job they should **get paid the same amount of money** no matter what their gender or race, or whether they have a disability or not. It shouldn't make any difference. In professional football, however, men often get paid more than women. **A lot** more!

Until early 2022, the US men's national team were earning **way more money** than the US women's national team. This was despite the fact that the women's team had won the FIFA Women's World Cup four times and the men's team had never even made it past the quarter-finals.

However, in Feburary 2022 the US women's team won a legal battle meaning they were **finally** going to be paid the same as the men's team. Yay!

This follows on from other countries such as **Brazil, Australia, Norway, New Zealand and the UK.** It's not something worldwide yet, but this shows there is hope.

The problem is that the prize money and wages for footballers all has to come from us. We are the people that buy the tickets, the shirts and pay to watch it on TV or online. So if we want women footballers to continue to be paid the same as men, **we need to put as much effort into supporting women's football as we do men's football.**

Hope Solo:
page 69

Lucy Bronze:
page 82

Megan Rapinoe:
page 76

Mia Hamm:
page 188

Power to everyone:
page 83

Becky Sellar:
page 124

How to watch
football on TV:
page 210

LUCY BRONZE

FOOTBALLING ERA:
2010s, 2020s.

DESCRIPTION:
A force on and off
the pitch.

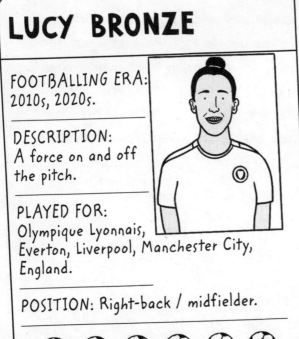

PLAYED FOR:
Olympique Lyonnais,
Everton, Liverpool, Manchester City,
England.

POSITION: Right-back / midfielder.

Famous for: Lucy is a great defender and a formidable tackler. But she is also a goal scorer, often scoring from outside the box.

Lucy started playing for the Sunderland under-12 team and then with their youth team. She won a scholarship to the University of North Carolina, where she played for the North Carolina Tar Heels.

Lucy has yet to win the World Cup for England but she played in the team that won the 2019 She Believes Tournament in the USA and came fourth in the 2019 FIFA Women's World Cup.

Power to everyone!

As well as paying women more, another solution to the problem of equal pay could be to stop paying the men quite so much money. Maybe FIFA should use some of the prize money it pays to support less rich sports.

We should celebrate anyone who is playing any sport regardless of their sex, gender, race or ability. And we need to make it as fair as we can for everyone, too.

One of the great things about sport is that it doesn't really matter how good you are. We tend to only see the best of the best being celebrated on TV and social media but anyone can have a go at any sport. It makes you feel happy when you do it and you'll make lots of new friends.

Who should be your footballing hero?

It's a great idea to have a footballing hero. You can find out all about them and do your best to be like them in certain ways.

I think the **best heroes** are people who were a bit like you when they were children, and then grew up to be successful and really **useful to the world** in some way.

So have a think about where you are at the moment.

If you can't afford decent football boots maybe you should think about Pelé or Diego Maradona for a hero. They both came from terrible **poverty** in the slums of South America.

Maybe you identify closely with your culture. Eusébio was one of the first **African-born footballing superstars.**

Perhaps you like to **stand up for others.** Megan Rapinoe uses her position as a footballer to protest against racial inequality. Marta is a goodwill ambassador for the United Nations. Johan Cruyff set up a foundation for impoverished children.

What **obstacles will you have to overcome** or maybe you are already overcoming? Zico and Lionel Messi had to overcome being smaller than average. Cristiano Ronaldo had to have heart surgery. Footballers with disabilities have to overcome their own difficulties every single day. Maybe one of them would be a powerful hero for you.

So have a look through this book and other books about football. Choose a hero and then go for it. Who knows what you'll become.

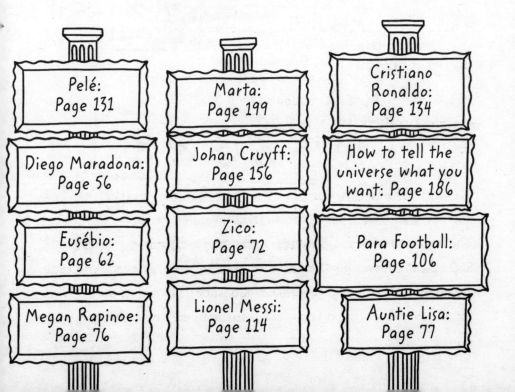

Pelé:
Page 131

Marta:
Page 199

Cristiano
Ronaldo:
Page 134

Diego Maradona:
Page 56

Johan Cruyff:
Page 156

How to tell the
universe what you
want: Page 186

Eusébio:
Page 62

Zico:
Page 72

Para Football:
Page 106

Megan Rapinoe:
Page 76

Lionel Messi:
Page 114

Auntie Lisa:
Page 77

LEV YASHIN

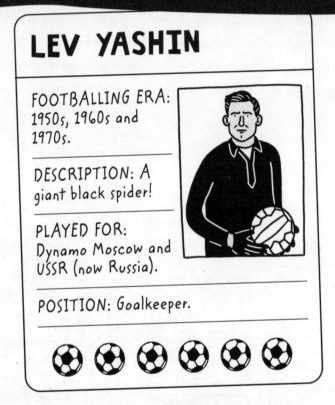

FOOTBALLING ERA: 1950s, 1960s and 1970s.

DESCRIPTION: A giant black spider!

PLAYED FOR: Dynamo Moscow and USSR (now Russia).

POSITION: Goalkeeper.

Famous for: Being the first goalkeeper to leave the goal line and organise his defenders. He was nicknamed the **'Black Spider'** because with his dark blue kit and his arms and legs flying in all directions he looked a bit like a black spider.

Random Fact: Yashin had a habit of spinning a huge web across the goal so that even when he couldn't get his hands on the ball, the web would bounce it out. He also caught hundreds of flies, beetles and a Brazilian centre-forward. Eventually, opposition teams found the only way they could get any shots past him was to catch him in a giant cup and take him out to the garden.

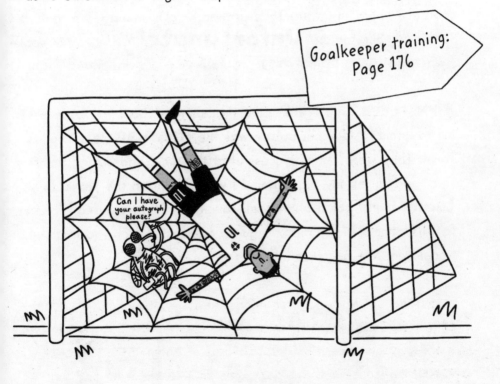

An interview with John Wark

John Wark played for Ipswich, Liverpool and Scotland in the 1970s and 1980s. It's **very difficult** to get to talk to most footballers, but my daughter's grandad Colin, managed to get John's number for me! **Unfortunately,** when we spoke I was also trying to look after my four-year-old daughter, Daphne.

JOHN: I got my big break aged sixteen when Bobby Robson asked me to come to Ipswich. Bobby was the **manager** of Ipswich Town. They were really successful at the time, and during the FA Cup I was given my big chance. I was playing in the **youth team** when I got a phone call saying that they needed a player for the quarter-finals match against Leeds. So I showed them what I could do. We beat Leeds 4–2.

ME: Hang on. My daughter needs the toilet. It's okay. I'll just take the phone in with me.

JOHN: Right.

ME: So what happened next? ...

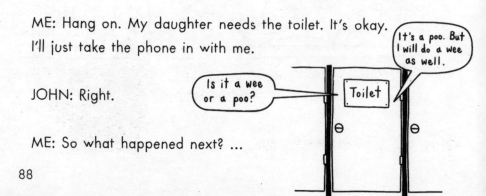

It's a poo. But I will do a wee as well.

Is it a wee or a poo?

Toilet

JOHN: Well, from then on I played for the Ipswich first team. I usually played as an **attacking defender.** I would come forward when the opposition wasn't expecting it and score. I was one of football's highest scoring defenders.

ME: How's the poo going?

DAPHNE: Nothing has come out yet.

JOHN: Erm ... Are you sure you don't want to phone me back?

ME: No, no, it's fine. How many goals did you score?

JOHN: Well, in one season I scored 36. And lots of them were penalties. Some footballers don't like penalties but I loved them. It's a chance to show what you're made of.

ME: Are you doing a poo or not?

ME: Well, thanks, John. It was nice to talk to you.

JOHN: Um ... yeah Thanks. Bye.

I think it was a ghost poo.

It's when you think you need a poo but then it turns out there was nothing there.

Scotland's unusual supporting style

I lived in Scotland for nearly ten years and still feel that I have left some part of myself behind there. Some of the great things about Scotland are the **cuisine,** the **weather** and the **midges** that will eat you alive if you're ever stood outside!

But my favourite thing about Scotland is the Scottish people's attitude to football. They are very **passionate** supporters! And when Scotland play England, the atmosphere can get **very** charged. Some Scottish people will often choose to support **any other team** over England.*

When England got knocked out of the European Cup by Germany, lots of Scottish people wore German football tops and **leather shorts** for a month. When Iceland beat England, some Scottish people wrote **songs** about it and learned **Icelandic.** Even if England played against a team of the **most evil** characters you can think of, some Scots would **still** cheer on the villains!

*This is obviously quite silly, and rivalry in sport can sometimes be problematic, unhelpful and even dangerous (when it moves out of the stands and into the real world). But when it's harmless, light-hearted fun allowing me to wear leather shorts, **I LOVE IT.**

Very evil football team

Speaking of baddies, the scariest, most spine-chilling team on the planet might look something like this:

The Dirty XI

MOST EVIL E UNITED

Manager

Substitutes

6	Dr. Evil
10	Bowser
20	Scar
21	Thanos
27	Mr. Burns
44	Feathers McGraw
52	Gru

Darth Vader from Star Wars - goalkeeper

Miss Trunchbull from Matilda - centre-half

Voldemort from the Harry Potter books - right-wing

Creek from Trolls - midfielder

The Child catcher from Chitty Chitty Bang Bang - sweeper

Mrs Coulter from His Dark Materials series - left-wing

Prince Hans of the Southern Isles from Frozen - striker

Mr O'Hare from The Lorax - striker

Al from Al's Toy Barn in Toy Story 2 - left-back

Cruella de Vil from 101 Dalmations - forward

Marjory Indent from my Boyface books - right-back

You'll notice that Darth Vader is in goal. I've put him there because he would just use the **force** to stop any balls from going over his line. There would, however, be an access shaft directly above his head and if you could bend a shot to drop just at the right moment, you could actually score a goal and explode the whole team of bad guys at the same time.

An interview with Graeme Le Saux

Graeme Le Saux played for England and Chelsea in the 1990s. He scored **lots of goals** and is now one of the **directors** of Real Mallorca. Luckily, he also plays five-a-side with my friend Mark, who got me his number. **Unfortunately,** when we spoke I was also trying to get my three children (Joe, Hayden and Daphne) ready to go for a walk and the two things may have got confused slightly.

ME: Hello, Graeme. Tell me how you **started** playing football.

GRAEME: As a kid I used to spend all day kicking the ball against the back wall of the house.

JOE: I can't find my walking boots.

HAYDEN: Just wear your wellies. Remember you lost your walking boots in a bog in Scotland.

GRAEME: If I hit the glass of the patio door my dad would come out and shout at me.

GRAEME: The game then was to kick the ball as close to the patio door as possible without hitting it.

ME: Can you guys keep the noise down? I'm trying to interview Graeme Le Saux!

GRAEME: I always wore socks. Otherwise your boots would rub against your feet.

DAPHNE: I don't want to wear socks.

ME: Why don't you want to wear socks?

GRAEME: Do you want to call me back another time?

DAPHNE: They are too wrinkly.

ME: No, it's fine. Can you tell me about the **way** you play football?

ME: But once you get your boots on, your socks will smooth out and you'll be fine.

GRAEME: Well, football is a great way to show the sort of person you are. For example, are you always going for glory? ...

GRAEME: ... Or do you **pass** well, looking out for others? ...

JOE: Are my boots on the wrong way round?

DAPHNE: Have you got the dog's poo bags?

GRAEME: ... Do you **dive** in front of shots to try and save them? ...

HAYDEN: Dad, Joe's boots are on the wrong feet.

GRAEME: ... how do you cope when you **lose**? ...

ME: Joe, take your boots off and start again.

DAPHNE: I don't want to go for a walk now. I want to watch Miraculous.

ME: Can you guys just be quiet for five minutes? I'm trying to interview Graeme Le Saux.

HAYDEN: Who is Graeme Lasso? Isn't that what cowboys have?

ME: I'm really sorry about this, Graeme. What's the **funniest goal** you've ever seen? And can you guys please just get out the back door?

DAPHNE: But I'm not wearing any shoes!

GRAEME: It has to be when Arsenal accidentally **chipped their own keeper.** At the time, Arsenal was a really boring team to watch, so when their right-back decided to hoof the ball back to David Seaman, the keeper, it was genuinely hilarious that Seaman was not really paying attention.

DAPHNE: Can I go to the loo before we go? It wasn't a ghost poo.

Own goals:
Page 144

Ridiculous goals:
Page 140

Strange things on club badges:
Page 212

Goalkeeper training:
Page 176

Footballer positions:
Page 151

Who should be your footballing hero?:
Page 84

The kit:
Page 48

Passing:
Page 162

Shooting:
Page 160

Tiny ball training drills:
Page 168

Stadiums

It's no good having a brilliant football team if people can't come and watch you play.

All over the world, clubs have built **huge buildings** that allow **thousands** of people to squeeze in and watch and cheer and chant and boo and love the game together.

It always takes ages to get into these places and going to the **toilet** in the middle of a match feels like it's taking forever. Mainly because you spend your whole wee hoping you don't miss a goal!

I once spent a whole match doing a poo. It was so **big** the commentators mentioned it on the TV.

It's unbelievable, Jeff.

It was very much a poo of two halves, Chris.

But anyway. Here are some of the most famous stadiums around the world.

Mascots: Page 200

Where is football played?: Page 18

Football match food: Page 111

Groundspeople: Page 198

WEMBLEY: London, UK

Known as the home of football, Wembley Stadium hosts many **championships** including the FA Cup, the UEFA Cup, the World Tiddlywinks Cup and the final of the **Bopping Dogs On The Head With Sausages** World Tournament.

If you've never played this sport before, you can find out more about it in *The Funny Life of Pets*. **But** basically, you get a dog. You get a sausage. You say 'Sit'. To the dog, not the sausage. You can't train a sausage.

Roll over!

I can't. I'm a sausage!

Then you have to throw the sausage and try and get it to bop your dog on the head. You get **ten points** if you manage it. What normally happens is that the dog catches and eats the sausage. And then the dog gets ten points. And a sausage.

Anyway – this all happens at Wembley Stadium. Every year. Usually on 31 June.

They also do football.

The beginning of the FA: Page 28

Bopping dogs on the head with sausages, in *The Funny Life of Pets*: Page 100

ALLIANZ: Munich, Germany

This stadium is really cool. It lights up as **two** different colours (red or blue) depending on who is playing there. This is because the venue is shared by two Munich teams – Bayern Munich and 1860 Munich.

Franz Beckenbauer: Page 150

If the two teams are playing each other it glows a weird **purple colour** that no one likes and they usually have a fight as to who gets the home dressing rooms.

WELCOME TO OLD TRAFFORD

THE THEATRE OF DREAMS

OLD TRAFFORD: Manchester, UK

This is somewhere you either **love** or **hate,** depending on whether you're a Manchester United supporter or not. You can't deny though there is always an amazing **atmosphere.**

This is because they have **special pumps** that force actual atmosphere into the stadium. Atmosphere that they have collected from exciting places around the world. If you sit in the stands at Old Trafford you are breathing air taken from pop concerts,

Disneyland and the Amazon rainforest, all blended together in a kind of **gassy soup.** It makes even the dullest nil-nil draw into one of the most exhilarating experiences of your life.

After each match, the remaining atmosphere is sucked into Kilner jars and sent to the Airedale Air Museum where it is kept forever in a special room or used to refill damaged footballs.

We have refilled this little beauty with the atmosphere from United vs City in 2012.

The Most Boring Thing In The World Paradox: Page 214

Other football positions named after household items: Page 218

Charity for damaged footballs: Page 204

Extra time: Page 145

CAMP NOU: Barcelona, Spain (Catalonia)

This is the biggest football stadium in Europe.

It was built in 1957 to replace the old stadium which had allowed supporters to sit on the walls with their **bums** hanging over the edge. This is why Barcelona fans are called *culés*.

*C*ulés is Catalan for 'Those who sit with their bums hanging out'.

I don't know **any** other language that has a word for that. Or anything like that. I hope though that somewhere in the world there is a language that has a word that means 'Those who don't load the dishwasher properly'.

I think that word should be Blumfanglers.

Ridiculous goals:
Page 140

Johan Cruyff:
Page 156

Free kicks:
Page 177

Lionel Messi:
Page 114

Diego
Maradona:
Page 56

ESTADIO AZTECA: Mexico City, Mexico

*W*ith a capacity of **104,000** this is the third biggest stadium in the world. It's the only stadium to have held two World Cup finals.

Unfortunately for English fans it is also where the infamous Hand of God incident took place.

Hand of God: Page 66

Unusual supporting style: Page 90

Handball: Page 130

The FIFA World Cup: Page 136

MY BACK GARDEN: Suffolk, UK

This stadium seats approximately eight people, but you could fit in a lot more if everyone brought their own deckchairs and beanbags.

At this infamous ground, potted plants have been **destroyed**, greenhouse panes have been **smashed** and my son Hayden played an entire match on his own against himself and then got **really angry** that he had lost. It took him about two years to realise that he couldn't really blame anyone but himself.

My footballing career continues!: Page 42

Who should be your footballing hero?: Page 84

Different ways of playing football: Page 36

SAN SIRO: Milan, Italy

This is the ground of arch-rivals AC Milan and Inter Milan.

I do like the idea of rivals having to **share** a home. It's a bit like making siblings share a bedroom. I bet the managers of AC and Inter have arguments about when to put the stadium **lights off** and who **farted** in the middle of the night.

Maybe world leaders who have arguments should also have to share a stadium, or a parliament building. Or go on holiday and share a twin bedroom in a caravan somewhere. For a **month.**

I reckon by the end of that month there would be trade agreements, world peace and the two would be **best friends** forever.

MARACANÃ: Rio de Janeiro, Brazil

Built to host the 1950 World Cup, this **whopper** of a stadium managed to fit in 199,000 people for the final between Brazil and Uruguay.

The atmosphere is amazing but the stadium does have a problem in that you can only park in the car park for an **hour.** This means that everyone has to nip out at half-time to put some more money in the machine. This is very annoying and badly thought out.

Zico:
Page 72

Pelé:
Page 131

Marta:
Page 199

LUSAIL ICONIC: Lusail, Qatar

This is the biggest of the stadiums built for the 2022 World Cup. It's designed to look like a traditional Arabian basket.

It's quite funny that they have named the stadium 'Iconic', which means something that has survived and been admired for a very **long** time. But the stadium is brand new.

I'm thinking I might change the title of this book to *The ICONIC Funny Life of Football* and also change my name to ...

James 'The Legend' Campbell.

Para Football

Para Football is a foundation and worldwide body of football for persons with disabilities. It has got nothing to do with parachuting. Although I have often thought that parachutes would make football much more entertaining – especially if the match was held on a really windy day.

People with disabilities tend to be quite different from one another so Para Football consists of teams and tournaments for the following:

- Amputee Football
- Blind Football
- Cerebral Palsy Football
- Deaf Football
- Down's Syndrome Football
- Dwarf Football

- Frame Football
- Intellectual Impairment Football
- Mental Health Football
- Allergic to Footballs Football
- Partially Sighted Football
- Powerchair Football

So whatever kind of brain or body you have, there is a type of football for you to compete in if you fancy it.

I can see my trampoline from here!

Powerchair Football

There are a few rule differences with Powerchair Football.

1. The ball is twice the size of a regular football. It has to be, otherwise it would get stuck under the wheelchairs' bumpers.

2. The goals don't have nets. They tried having nets and people kept getting their wheels tangled up in them.

3. Before the match starts, all players line up and race from one end of the pitch to the other. If anyone's chair is faster than the others, their engine gets tuned down so they don't have an unfair advantage.

Different ways of playing football: Page 36

Football at school

School is a great place to play football.

A lot of children spend the **whole** of lunchtime playing football. Even the bit when they are eating their lunch. They just **balance** their plate of macaroni cheese on their head and carry on. Goalkeepers put their main course behind one post and their pudding behind the other. Each time they have to dive to their left or their right, they take a **quick spoonful** of beef stew or a **cheeky mouthful** of pink sponge accordingly.

Lunchtime football is usually very disorganised. No one knows who is on whose team, what the score is and there is very rarely a referee.

Sometimes, someone will shout 'BUNDLE!' and everyone will pile on top of each other until there is a **massive mound** of kids in the middle of the field and the teachers will have to untie children's legs from other children's legs and drag them to one side. Then everyone will have **faces** the colour of Barbie's car and one flat child will be found at the bottom looking like a **sweaty tortilla pancake.** Then the head teacher will spend the whole of assembly telling everyone that football is **banned** until people can stop bundling on top of each other. But the head teacher will mispronounce the word bundle because they are 112 years old and haven't **bundled** on top of anyone since the Second World War and actually tells everyone to stop **bungling,** so everyone wants to laugh but they can't because they know if they do they will get a detention for the whole **rest of the day.**

The beginning of my footballing career: Page 30

Playground rules: Page 112

The history of the kit: Page 50

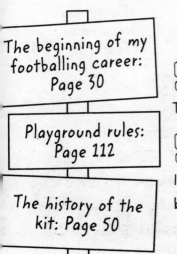

You will also play football as part of PE. This will be a lot more organised.

You might end up in the school team. I don't know anything about this really because I was never picked.

Kids' football clubs

If you really like football you might also want to play in a **local team** that is not connected to your school.

You'll be expected to be there **every** weekend – usually on a Saturday morning. It doesn't matter what the weather is doing either so don't be surprised if you find yourself training in the middle of a **hurricane.**

If this happens do not **swap shirts** with anyone on the pitch. As you're in the middle of taking your shirt off the wind will catch you like a kite and you'll go floating over the goalposts and into someone's garden.

Please can we have our defender back?

League table of picnic ruinations: Page 222

Scotland's unusual supporting style: Page 90

How to watch football on TV: Page 210

Football match food

The entertainment at a football match may be top-notch, but often the food is **terrible.**

It reminds me of school lunches and the mystery of school lunch servers. Why give the job to people who clearly don't care about food? You wouldn't let people who didn't like children become teachers would you? Or maybe that's not a good example ...

Anyway – for some reason, football bosses will spend **£20 million** on a new striker but won't spend more than a few pence on the half-time food.

Classic football food includes:

- Meat pies that look like cat poo in pastry.

- Cheesy chips which are actually just a slice of cheese on top of some chips.

- Dead squirrel on a stick.

- Manky bum pie.

Stadiums: Page 98

Equal pay Page 80

Playground rules

Football played in the playground at school has slightly different rules.

1. **T**here are two captains. These are usually the **oldest** or **biggest** or **best** at football.

2. **T**he captains choose teams. Don't worry if you are always chosen last. One day you'll be able to get your **revenge** by training an army of purple monkeys and using them to take over the world!

3. **T**he goalkeeper is usually the **smallest / worst** player on the team, but if the other team get a penalty, your captain will immediately sack the goalkeeper and try to save it themselves.

4. **T**here should be no difference in the way that the players dress so it is **impossible** to remember who is on your team. Don't worry. Whenever you have the ball, your team will scream things at you like, 'I'm in space!', 'Stop hogging the ball!' and 'You have got pink sponge all over your face!'.

5. The game will start immediately - and finish when the bell goes.

6. Some matches might last a whole week and there will be arguments over what the score is. These arguments should be settled through more football.

7. There are **no edges** to the pitch. It stretches out as far as anyone can be bothered to meander.

8. If there are **no proper goals** you can use a pile of coats and jumpers. All piles should grow inwards to make the goal smaller.

9. There is **no offside** because no one really knows what offside means. Goal-hanging, however, is to be discouraged.

10. If you score a goal you will not only have to celebrate but will also have to make the noise of the crowd cheering. Nobody else cares about your goal.

LIONEL MESSI

FOOTBALLING ERA:
2003 onwards.

DESCRIPTION:
Loyal leader.

PLAYS FOR:
Barcelona and
Argentina.

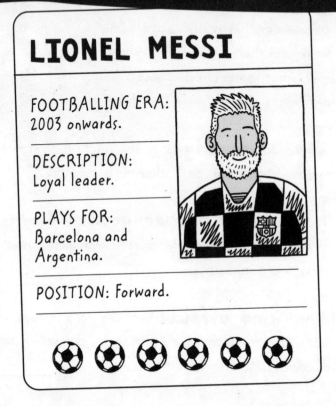

POSITION: Forward.

Famous for: Being one of the greatest footballers ever. Messi was born in Argentina then moved to Barcelona aged just thirteen to join their junior team. He was incredibly talented but had a **medical condition** that meant he didn't grow properly.

Luckily, Barcelona paid for really expensive treatment to help him. I think they might also have injected some sort of **magic** into his bones because by the age of sixteen Messi was Barcelona's youngest ever goal scorer, and now holds the record for the most number of goals scored in a calendar year – 91.

Bonus stuff: Whenever Messi scores a goal, he **points to the sky** to remember his grandmother who helped him with his football when he was a little boy.

Random fact: Mr Messi is one of only four footballers who are named after **Mr Men characters.** The other three are Ian Rush, Geoff Strong and Peter Crouch (Mr Tall).

Hello!

Goal celebrations:
Page 142

Who should be your footballing hero?:
Page 84

Shooting:
Page 160

The referee

The referee is in charge of making sure that all the players are following the **rules.**

If you have been reading this book and thinking to yourself, 'Hmmm, I like the sound of this football thing but maybe I'd like to be in charge of it instead of playing it', then maybe you should think about being a referee.

Another test is to think about these questions. If you answer **yes** to any of these questions you should probably become a ref.

1. Do you love football but prefer to avoid touching the ball?

2. Maybe when you play football, you never get passed to? Referees only get passed the ball by mistake.

3. Do you like the idea of having to get out of the way of the ball when it's coming at you really quickly?

4. Are you really good at calming people down?

5. Is your idea of fun running backwards and forwards in terrible weather for no real reason whatsoever?

6. Do you have your own whistle?

Rules you didn't know existed

If you're going to play football, it's important to know **the rules.** You don't want to spend all week dreaming up a brilliant plan to distract the striker you're marking by pouring **jelly** down their shirt only to find out that there's a rule that says you're **not allowed** to bring food on to the pitch.

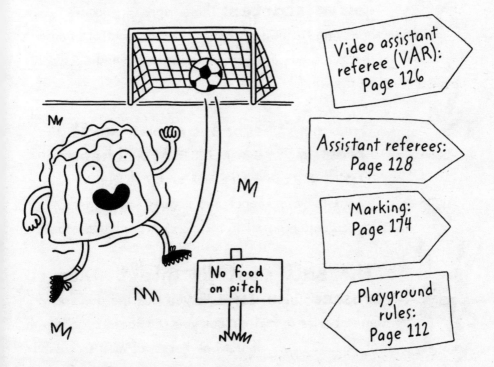

No food on pitch

Video assistant referee (VAR): Page 126

Assistant referees: Page 128

Marking: Page 174

Playground rules: Page 112

There are some rules, however, that don't get used very often at all. Here are a few.

Six second rule: Goalkeepers are only allowed to hold the ball for **six seconds.** After that they have to kick it or throw it to someone else. You may have a similar rule for food that has landed on the kitchen floor.

You can get sent off before you've started: That's right. If you are really annoying to the referee you can be sent off before the game has even started! So don't wind up the ref in the tunnel.

You can't score an own goal from a free kick or a throw-in: If you use a free kick or a throw-in to pass back to your keeper and it goes wrong and accidentally lands in the goal, it does not count.

The ball must be intact when it crosses the line: If you kick the ball so hard that it bursts in mid-air but you still score a goal with it, it doesn't count. If the ball bursts after it's crossed the line however, that's fine and is an actual goal.

The offside rule

One of **the most famous** of all football rules is the offside rule. It's famous because it's really hard to explain and some people find it even harder to understand.

Some of these people are referees and assistant referees.

My grandpa used to explain the offside rule at dinner using salt and pepper pots, gravy boats and a jug of Ribena. Thinking about it, my grandpa used to explain **everything** using objects on the **kitchen table.** For my whole life I have only been able to understand things like radar, anti-lock brakes and long division in terms of mugs, tumblers and jars of pickled beetroot.

Allow me then to explain the **offside rule,** beginning with a very helpful diagram ...

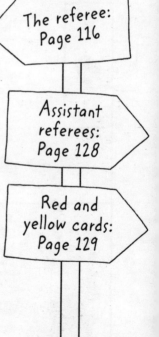

The referee:
Page 116

Assistant referees:
Page 128

Red and yellow cards:
Page 129

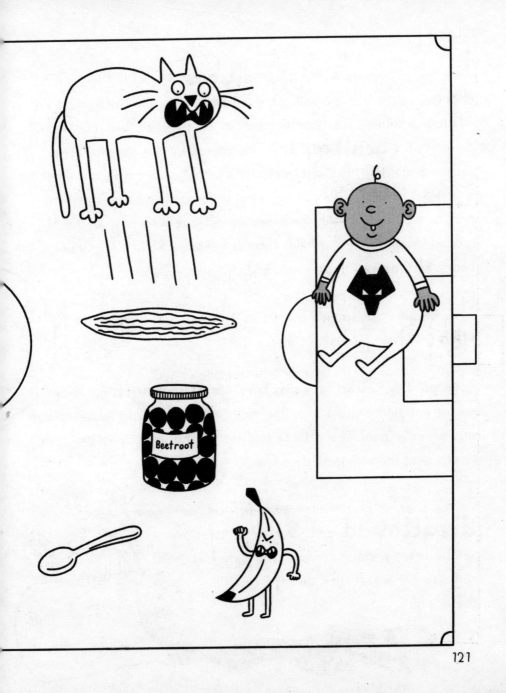

Imagine your plate is the **opposition's goal.** The **defenders** are the salt, pepper, gravy and glass of water. The jug of Ribena is a **forward** and it's offside because it's closer to the **goalkeeper** (represented by the burned bit of roast potato) than the **defenders** are. Just because the Ribena is offside, however, doesn't necessarily mean it is doing anything against the rules. It only becomes an offence when the bottle of tomato ketchup (the midfield wizard) kicks the ball (a scrunched-up bunch of Quality Street wrappers).

The offside rule sounds a lot simpler when you understand **what the point** of it is.

The point is to stop forwards from **goal-hanging,** which means hanging around near the opposite goal hoping to get a pass and an easy goal. The offside rule means that you can't be closer to the goal than the last defender.

If you score a goal while you're offside, your goal will be **disallowed** and your jar of beetroot will be taken away from you. The defenders will also get a free kick and the rest of the gravy.

Gravy

The most important rule of course is that if you are explaining the offside rule during dinner, **no one** is allowed to use or eat any of the things that you are using as part of your explanation. I once accidentally moved a jar of pickled onions because it was in the way of my elbow and this caused my auntie's reading glasses to be no longer offside. Grandpa was very annoyed about this and gave me a jar of yellow-card mustard.

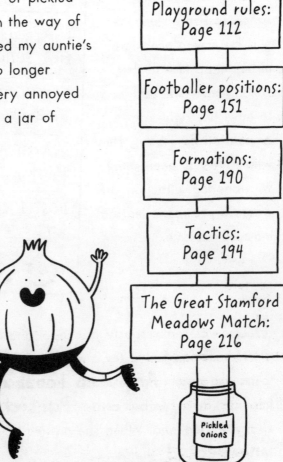

Playground rules:
Page 112

Footballer positions:
Page 151

Formations:
Page 190

Tactics:
Page 194

The Great Stamford
Meadows Match:
Page 216

GREAT PLAYERS OF ALL TIME

Famous for: Becky Sellar is an awesome Amputee Footballer. She was born with problems in her hip and right leg, which meant she had to have her right leg amputated as a baby. Her whole life has been spent with one leg, although she wears a prosthetic leg most of the time.

Becky Sellar

FOOTBALLING ERA: 2010s, 2020s

DESCRIPTION: Wonder Woman.

PLAYS FOR: Partick Thistle.

POSITION: Centre-forward.

⚽ ⚽ ⚽ ⚽ ⚽ ⚽

Becky was really sporty at school and her teachers were great at encouraging her to try anything. As a grown-up Becky decided to have a go at **Amputee Football** and went along to her local Para Football club - **Partick Thistle,** which is in Glasgow, Scotland. When she arrived however, she found out two **unexpected** things ...

1. You're not allowed to wear your prosthetic leg in Amputee Football. This would be the first time in ages that she had been out in public without it!

2. Every single other person on the team was a **man!**

I spoke to Becky on the phone and she says that she was always used to being the **odd one out.** Usually, she's the only person with a disability in a group. With Amputee Football, everyone playing had a disability but she wasthe only woman. She didn't care though, and got stuck in.

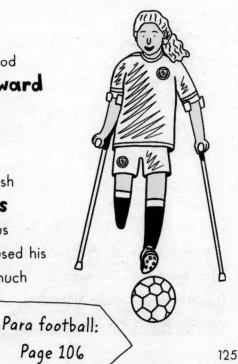

Soon, she showed she was good enough to be a **centre-forward** for the team.

Becky Sellar's heroes include **Rachel Corsie** (the Scottish women's captain) and **Marcus Rashford.** She likes Marcus because, she told me, 'He has used his fame and talent to achieve so much for other people'.

Para football: Page 106

Video assistant referee (VAR)

One of the **worst** things in football is when the referee makes the **wrong decision.** Everyone can see it was handball but the ref allowed the goal. The player was obviously onside but the assistant referee called it wrong. There was definitely an **alien spaceship** that landed in the middle of the pitch but the referee just didn't see it for some reason.

The Video Assistant Referee, or VAR, was brought in to help with all this. VAR is a team of people who check the footage from loads of video cameras to see if the referee has made any wrong decisions.

I think they should also start using VAR in school playgrounds so that if a **fight** breaks out your teachers can look at the video and see **who started it.**

They always say it doesn't matter who started it. **But it does!**

Because the person who DIDN'T start it (which is almost certainly – YOU) is the person who didn't do anything wrong.

Although if someone starts a fight with you it's probably still wrong to fight back. But that's for another book called: *The Funny Life of Ethics* which I have no intention of writing.

If you have any thoughts on the morals of playground fights then please email at: seriouslyisaidiwasntgoingtowritethatbook@canyoujustgoandplayforabit.com

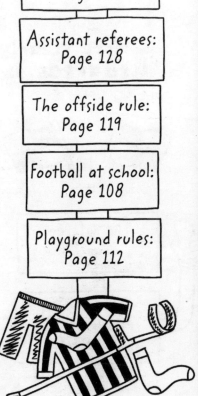

The referee:
Page 116

Assistant referees:
Page 128

The offside rule:
Page 119

Football at school:
Page 108

Playground rules:
Page 112

Assistant referees

It's the assistant referee's job to make decisions when they can see **more clearly** than the referee. But, if the referee **disagrees,** they are allowed to overrule them.

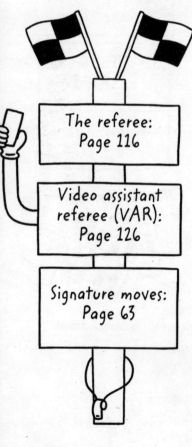

The referee:
Page 116

Video assistant referee (VAR):
Page 126

Signature moves:
Page 63

This is very similar to what goes on between me and my daughter when we go into town after school. I am allowed to make some decisions about things like which shops we are going to and where we will go for cake. But only if the decisions I make agree exactly with what she decided before the conversation started. It's great because this way she gets what she wants, and I get to pretend that I am in charge.

Red and yellow cards

Referees have three types of cards:

- Yellow cards

- Red cards

- Cards with their contact details in case they make friends with someone during the match

That was never offside ref!

I am awarding a free kick against you, but I think you are really cool. Maybe we can exchange details and go and get a milkshake together sometime?

The yellow card is like a warning. If you foul someone, accidentally bring your pet Labrador on to the pitch, fart in the referee's general direction or shout 'Bumpackets!' at the opposition's goalkeeper, then the referee will probably show you a yellow card.

If you do something bad again then you will get a red card and have to go home immediately. Your team then has to carry on without you – with just ten players!

So leave your Labrador at home!

The offside rule: Page 119

League table of picnic ruinations: Page 222

Handball

You are not allowed to **touch** the ball with your **hand** or **arm.** Even by accident. If you do, the other team get a free kick.

Goalkeepers can use their hands, but only in their own area. They cannot pick the ball up, run to the other end of the pitch and throw it into the other team's goal.

That's how **American Football** works.

Different ways of playing football Page 36

In back garden football, your grown-up is allowed to use their hand to stop it hitting them in the face. This is an instinctive **grown-up-reaction** and no free kick can be awarded.

If you are under the age of five, you are allowed to pick the ball up and put it somewhere slightly different before kicking it. If anyone calls handball then you are allowed to chuck the ball in the pond whilst yelling,

I don't want to play your stupid game anyway! Now look! It's a mermaid ball for mermaids!

PELÉ

FOOTBALLING ERA:
1960s and 1970s.

DESCRIPTION:
Smiley Brazilian
man, usually with
a football glued to
his foot with magic.

PLAYED FOR: Santos
and Brazil.

POSITION: Forward.

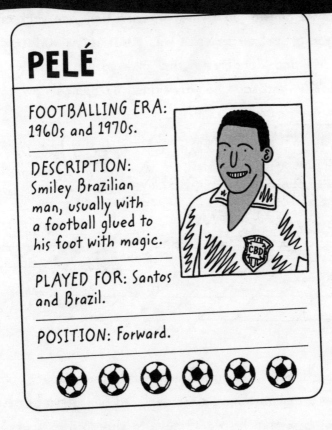

Famous for: Being probably **the most famous**
footballer of all time. Across the world, the word 'Pelé' is actually
more recognisable than the word 'Coca-Cola'!

When he was a child, Pelé couldn't afford an actual football so he used a sock stuffed with newspaper or a **grapefruit.** This meant he had to play whilst wearing only one sock and being chased by a grapefruit seller. It was **running away** from greengrocers and launderettes that allowed him to develop his dribbling skills, and soon he was signed by Santos.

Lots of European teams tried to buy Pelé from Santos, but in 1961 the Brazilian government declared him a **national treasure** so that he would have to stay in Brazil.

You could try to use this excuse to stop people making you go somewhere you don't want to go.

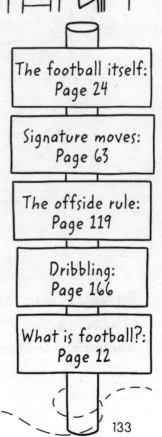

Come on. We need to go to the supermarket to get some grapefruit.

I'm afraid I can't come to the supermarket because I am a national treasure.

One of Pelé's signature moves was the **Drible da Vaca**, which is when you don't actually touch the ball but let it run on. This really **confuses** defenders and often the ball rolls right past them, allowing you to dodge past while they flail on the floor.

I often do this by mistake. I try to kick the ball but I miss it completely and **fall over.** When people laugh at me I just tell them I was practising my *Drible da Vaca*. Unfortunately, the way I pronounce Portuguese is so terrible that what I actually say translates as **'I am dribbling like a cow'.**

The football itself: Page 24

Signature moves: Page 63

The offside rule: Page 119

Dribbling: Page 166

What is football?: Page 12

CRISTIANO RONALDO

FOOTBALLING ERA:
2000s onwards.

DESCRIPTION:
Shiny robot-athlete.

PLAYED FOR:
Manchester United,
Real Madrid,
Juventus and Portugal.

POSITION: Forward.

Famous for: Being like some sort of **footballing machine.** Ronaldo famously keeps to a fitness regime that no other mortal could manage. He has a cryogenic chamber in his house so he can **freeze himself** after matches and training! He has his own doctor, nutritionist and chef following him around all the time to make sure he eats exactly what he's supposed to and doesn't **accidentally scoff a chocolate brownie** when no one is looking.

Ronaldo has scored so many goals that he has actually scored more goals with his left (weaker) foot than most strikers have scored with their best foot. He can **jump** higher than most basketball players and kangaroos.

Who should be your footballing hero?: Page 84

He also always seems to be in the right place at the right time. Scientists reckon that he has a super ability to be able to see three seconds into the **future.**

Bonus stuff: As a teenager he was diagnosed with a heart defect and had to have surgery. The doctors may have accidentally given him **superpowers.** In any event, Ronaldo was back training three days later.

Ronaldo shows me that one of the ways to be the best in the world at something is to take it too seriously. **Become a machine.** I think that's what happened to my dishwasher. It started off as a small, rectangular man who washed dishes so obsessively that he turned into a shiny metal dishwasher!

The FIFA World Cup

There are two World Cups. One for men and one for women. There has been talk of having a World Cup for mermaids but I think that's a silly idea as **mermaids** have fins instead of feet.

It shouldn't really be called the World Cup because you don't win a cup. You win a trophy.

It's not even cup shape. Really the tournament should be called the **FIFA World Blobby Gold Thing.**

You're beautiful!

The thirty-two teams that enter the tournament gradually get whittled down to just two, who will **battle** it out in the World Cup final. The winning team become **world champions** and they are allowed to take their shirts off and run around the pitch, wrapping themselves in flags, crying with happiness for literally four days.

Goal celebrations:
Page 142

Football leagues:
Page 34

Football at
the Olympics:
Page 138

Match-fixing:
Page 202

The Great Stamford
Meadows Match:
Page 216

How to tell the
universe what you
want: Page 186

Football at the Olympics

The Olympic Games is arguably the **greatest sporting event** in the world, but FIFA have always been very keen that Olympic Football shouldn't be seen as more important than the World Cup.

In 1932, for example, FIFA made sure that there was no football at the Olympics by **rolling up** the football pitch and hiding it.

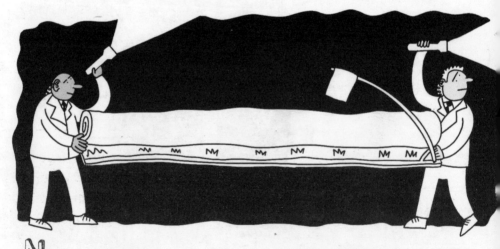

Not every footballer is even allowed to play in the Olympics. For most of the 20th century, only amateurs were allowed to play. And these days the rules are **so complicated** that I have fallen asleep **three times** trying to understand them.

Basically, you have to be under twenty-three years old, apart from **three** of you who can be as old as you like – unless you are women in which case you can all be **any** age you like, which means the women's Olympic Football is of the same level as the World Cup.

But if it's a Tuesday you have to wear **three pairs of socks** and if one of your team doesn't like **spaghetti** you have to play football on the same pitch as the javelin – **at the same time.**

Ugh. I hate spaghetti.

The FIFA World Cup: Page 136

Rules you didn't know existed: Page 117

Who plays football?: Page 14

Where is football played?: Page 18

Stadiums: Page 98

Mascots: Page 200

Ridiculous goals

Sometimes goals happen in ridiculous ways.

My favourite ones are when the goalkeeper **falls over.** Or when the ball does something unexpected like hit a bump in the pitch and go in a different direction. It's also extremely funny when the goalkeeper kicks the ball out and it accidentally bounces off a striker's **face** and goes into the goal.

I think there should be a **special statistic** for goals scored with faces.

Can you imagine how that would feel? At first you'd be really upset because you've just had a ball kicked in your face. And then you'd realise that everyone is cheering and the ball is in the back of the net. You have scored! **With your face!**

Scoring a goal is **not the only thing** you can accidentally do with your face.

You can also:

- Accidentally close the fridge – with your face.

- Accidentally stroke an over-enthusiastic golden retriever – with your face.

- Accidentally scare your hamster back into its little hamster-home – with your face.

- Accidentally do a sarcastic face when your parents ask you to unload the dishwasher – with your face.

- Accidentally unload the dishwasher – with your face.

Signature moves: Page 63

League table of picnic ruinations: Page 222

Red and yellow cards: Page 129

Goal celebrations: Page 142

Johan Cruyff: Page 156

Shooting: Page 160

Goal celebrations

A goal is the **most important** thing that happens on a football pitch, so it's important that everyone **celebrates.**

If you are the scorer you have to run in a random direction and then all your teammates will **chase** you and **pile** on top of your head.

I think this sort of celebration should happen in regular life. If someone in your family makes a really good fish pie you should all pile on top of them after lunch. **Or** if someone in your class gets **100 per cent** in a test you should all run around whooping and then take turns to pour water on their face.

If you get a chance before your teammates pile on top of you, you should do some sort of dance for your fans and admirers.

These dances might include:

- Rubbing your bum along the ground like a dog with worms
- The Robot
- Some sort of terrible samba
- Dabbing
- Pointing to the sky
- Taking your boot off and using it to pretend to phone your parents
- Taking your shorts off and running around in your pants
- Sliding on your knees like you used to do on the shiny floor of the assembly hall until you got told off.

I tend to celebrate goals scored in the garden by pulling my shirt over my face and accidentally running into the **compost bin.**

Goals I have scored in proper football matches are a lot more rare so I tend to celebrate them by taking a week off and spending some time by the sea, writing poems and thinking about how my attitude to love has changed as I've got older.

Own goals

What is the **most embarrassing** thing you can do on a football pitch?

Is it to miss a penalty by hoofing the ball so high that it is in danger of disrupting a domestic aeroplane flight?

Oi!

Gary Lineker pooed himself: Page 40

Or is it having a bottom-based accident in your shorts?

No. The most embarrassing thing you can do on a football pitch is accidentally score a goal in the **wrong net!**

Own goals are the **worst!** Especially if you score them with your face.

If it happens to you, all you can do is try and make up for it with some awesome play. Or just run off the pitch, jump on to the back of a donkey and ask it to take you somewhere very far away.

Ridiculous goals: Page 140

Kids' football clubs: Page 110

Signature moves: Page 63

Shooting: Page 160

Extra time

In most football matches you get points for winning or drawing. But in big competitions, like the FA Cup, there are matches where someone has to **win** no matter what.

If one of these matches ends in a draw, it goes into **extra time** and they play two more halves of 15 minutes each. This is **hard work** for the players because they have already been playing as hard as they can for an hour and a half.

Mistakes get made. Secret **kittens** fall out of players' pockets and everyone looks sweaty and fed up.

At the end of extra time whoever is winning is now the winner. But – sometimes the score is still level. **There is still a deadlock!** Then the game goes to **penalties** which are even more nerve-racking and exciting.

Saving a penalty is the **greatest thing** a goalkeeper can do. Missing a penalty is one of the **worst things** a player can do. However, though it can make them feel down in the dumps, it often drives them to want to play even better in future matches.

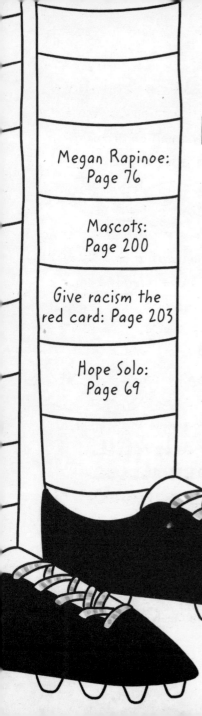

Megan Rapinoe:
Page 76

Mascots:
Page 200

Give racism the
red card: Page 203

Hope Solo:
Page 69

Football pride

LGBTQ+ stands for lesbian, gay, bisexual, transgender, queer (or questioning) and many others shown in the +. These are all different words people use to **identify themselves** in relation to who they do or don't love or fancy, or what gender they are. Unfortunately some of these people face discrimination (unfair treatment) for identifying as part of these groups. This is a problem in football too, which is **ridiculous** because people who identify as LGBTQ+ are just as likely to want to play football as anyone else. They should **never** feel like they can't.

To try and fix this problem, footballers, fans and other industry folk are trying to **raise awareness** of the issue to stamp it out for good.

One **campaign** involves getting players to **wear rainbow laces** as a symbol of **inclusion.** I would get some myself but knowing me I'd just spend the whole game looking at my colourful feet and fall flat on my face. So perhaps I could wear a rainbow hat instead.

Despite these efforts, lots of players still experience abuse because of how they identify. That's why you have to make sure you **never** do this. Never ever. And if you ever see anyone doing it, use your rainbow laces to form a lasso to stop them **immediately.**

If you do want to shout stuff at players, there are plenty of non-abusive things you can shout instead. I like to go to football matches and shout **the names of different condiments.**

It doesn't help the team I'm shouting at, but it does mean I leave the football match with lots of sachets of ketchup, mayonnaise and mustard.

KETCHUP!

MAYONNAISE!

MUSTARD!

Football match food: Page 110

Caps

In the 19th century, all football players had to wear a cap during matches. The rule got dropped quite quickly though because everyone's cap kept **falling off** and getting trodden on. Also, some players were using the cap as a sneaky place to keep **sandwiches** and their collection of **secret pet kittens.**

In 1903, Charlie Roberts (who played for Manchester United) was accused of keeping a fully grown cat under his cap, and some people claimed the **cat** was telling him how and where to kick the ball!

Footballers no longer have to wear caps, but the number of times a player has played for a particular team is still measured in terms of caps. Every time you play for **your country** you get given an actual cap as a **souvenir.**

Stadiums: Old Trafford: Page 100

Cristiano Ronaldo currently has **167 caps** from playing for Portugal, which is a world record. Portugal also gives all its players a box of those lovely custard tarts they make so well, a bottle of lemonade with their name on it and a pack of football stickers.

My team – Stewmarket Inter-dimensional Wanderers – gives each of its players a **time-travelling helmet,** a tiny piece of **meteorite** and a **special set of underwear** in case you poo yourself whilst tunnelling through different dimensions.

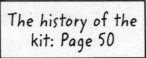

Gary Lineker pooed himself: Page 40

Stewmarket Inter-dimensional Wanderers: Page 230

Inter-dimensional Football explained: Page 44

Cristiano Ronaldo: Page 134

The history of the kit: Page 50

Extra time: Page 145

Corners: Page 180

FRANZ BECKENBAUER

FOOTBALLING ERA:
1960s and 1970s.

DESCRIPTION:
Woolly-headed
warrior.

PLAYED FOR:
Bayern Munich and
West Germany.

POSITION: Sweeper.

Famous for:
Being the greatest
German player ever.
Beckenbauer scored
fourteen goals in three
World Cups, and pretty
much **invented** a
new position called
the **sweeper.** He
would play behind
the defensive line,
sweeping up any
ball that got past.
He didn't, of course,
carry an actual
broom. That would
be silly and against the rules.

Brilliant stat: After he retired as a player, Beckenbauer
was made manager for Germany. When they won the World Cup
in 1990, he became one of only three men to have won the World
Cup as both a player and as a manager.

Footballer positions

When you are little there are only two positions you can play – goalkeeper, or **chasing the ball wherever it is.** But as you get better you might find that you are asked to stay in a particular position.

Here are some of the positions you might be asked to play:

THE STRIKER usually stays close to the goal and aims to **score** as much as possible. Often strikers are able to just tap the ball in by sticking a foot out, but will then celebrate wildly for half an hour. Do not get confused with strikers who **go on strike from work** or school to **protest** about climate change.

Climate change is worse than homework.

Shooting: Page 160

Goal celebrations: Page 142

Ridiculous goals: Page 140

THE WINGER has the job of **running up and down** the sidelines. It's their job to cross the ball in towards the striker. Do not get confused with a **Wing Man.** That is a friend who stands next to you while you try to impress someone you fancy. It's their job to make you look **cool.**

Number 9 is a really good listener and he loves animals too.

THE MIDFIELDERS spend most of their time in the middle of the pitch. People say that games are **won or lost** in the midfield. Which is strange because there are no goals there. But I think it means that good midfielders will **block** the other team, and help their team to score goals. Do not get confused with **FIELDERS.** These are strange people who play something called cricket, which mainly involves standing on your

own on a big field watching something miles away and occasionally having to pick up a tiny red ball and throw it back.

THE DEFENSIVE MIDFIELDER supports the defence by **filling the hole** between midfielders and the main defenders. They also tend to be really defensive about everything.

THE ATTACKING MIDFIELDER makes runs towards the goal, chips balls in for the strikers and generally entertains the crowd.

Do not confuse with **Atta King Midfielder.** This was a man who lived in the swamps off the coast of Costa Rica who thought he was king. He's called Midfielder because he was born in the middle of a field.

THE DEFENDERS tend to stay near their own goal and it's their job to **stop** the other team scoring. Sometimes they get to take the ball up the field, but once they've kicked it to a forward they have to go running back to their **keeper** who is often very annoyed with them and demands to know where they have been for the last sixty seconds.

Diego Maradona: Page 56

Graeme Souness: Page 47

Free kicks: Page 177

Auntie Lisa: Page 77

keeper has left the chat.

THE GOALKEEPERS are people who have gone to the trouble of buying their own **gloves.** They have not nicked their parent's gardening gloves and half-filled them with sand to make it look like they have **massive hands.** Goalkeepers very rarely score goals, **but** they do get the chance to make saves. My grandpa used to say that a penny saved was as good as a penny earned, so maybe he would also have said that a goal saved is as good a goal scored.

Mind you, he also said there were winged creatures living under the stairs and that Mrs Pearson from number 17 was a **yeti.** So it's probably best not to listen to him.

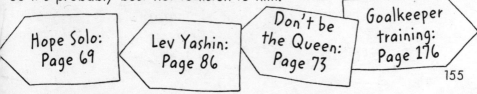

The offside rule: Page 119

Tactics: Page 194

Hope Solo: Page 69

Lev Yashin: Page 86

Don't be the Queen: Page 73

Goalkeeper training: Page 176

JOHAN CRUYFF

FOOTBALLING ERA: 1960s, 1970s and 1980s.

DESCRIPTION: A rebel wearing the number 14 on his top.

PLAYED FOR: Ajax, Barcelona and the Netherlands.

POSITION: Attacking midfielder / forward.

Famous for: Being the greatest Dutch player of all time and inventing the Cruyff Turn.

Signature moves: Page 63

Cruyff saw the game as **entertainment.** It was more important to him that people enjoyed watching his team play than it was for him to win. Despite this, his teams did an awful lot of winning.

Bonus stuff: Cruyff was an expert in something called **Total Football.** Teams that play Total Football can change positions throughout the match. Defenders can attack and attackers can swap around. This can make it very **confusing** for their opposition.

I do a similar thing when I'm loading the dishwasher. I call it **Total Dishwashing.** Sometimes I put the cups where the plates should go and the cutlery where the cups should be. This confuses the dishwasher and makes it really difficult for the thing to know what's going to happen next. One day I will beat it!

Football at school:
Page 108

Free kicks:
Page 177

Ridiculous goals:
Page 140

Goal celebrations:
Page 142

Ball control

It doesn't matter how far you can kick a ball; you need to be able to **control** it as well. It's really embarrassing when someone passes to you, you miss the ball and it lands in someone's **picnic.** (Having a football land in your pork pie is the second most common cause of a ruined picnic.)

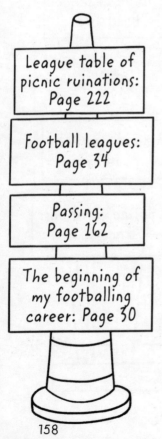

League table of picnic ruinations: Page 222

Football leagues: Page 34

Passing: Page 162

The beginning of my footballing career: Page 30

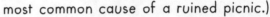

Learn to cushion the ball with the side of your foot so it stops in front of you. Or use the bottom of your foot to trap the ball if it's coming at you in a bouncy way. This technique does not work on **bouncy golden retrievers.** There is no defence against an over-enthusiastic golden retriever. I'm surprised more of them don't play in the Premiership.

This is also why 'Someone else's golden retriever' is in the league table of why picnics are ruined.

Shielding

This means protecting the ball from the opposition. Try sticking your arms out and leaning back so the defender can't get close enough to the ball to kick it. It's **not a foul** as long as you don't grab their shirt or poke them in the belly button. Belly button poking is very much frowned upon by the referee and very much squealed upon by whoever is having their belly button poked.

Another way to shield the ball is to use an **actual shield.** Mine is made of wood and weighs almost as much as I do, so it is tricky to play with but no one wants to come to tackle me when I have it. I think the **sword** helps too.

Red and yellow cards: Page 129

Playground rules: Page 112

Rules you didn't know existed: Page 117

The history of the kit: Page 50

Shooting

This is when you kick the ball as **hard** as you can, aiming for a place inside the goal where the goalkeeper is not.

A few things to remember:

1. Make sure the ankle of your kicking foot is locked and solid. Imagine your leg and foot is **Thor's hammer!**

2. Lean **forward** over the ball. If you lean back, the ball will fly over the crossbar and into someone's garden.

3. The **faster** you run towards the ball, the harder you will kick it.

4. Kick the centre of the ball. If you hit the bottom you will get backspin which slows the ball down. If it's raining it will

also send **water** spraying into your eyes and then you won't notice if a bird swoops down on you and tries to steal your hair to make a nest with.

5. In a match, everything goes a lot more quickly. So practise shooting from awkward places and in a hurry. I spend a lot of time in the garden trying to kick the ball at the shed whilst my daughter **sits on my head** and farts on the back of my neck like a **pongy scarf.**

Different ways of playing football: Page 36

Football at school: Page 108

Goal celebrations: Page 142

Kids' football clubs: Page 110

My footballing career continues!: Page 42

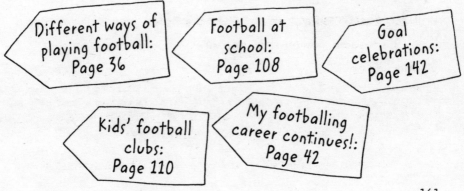

Passing

You might feel like you're Lionel Messi and can **dribble** the length of the pitch and score but it's really unlikely. (Unless of course you are Lionel Messi in which case, 'Hello Lionel! Can you *please* return that mermaid costume I lent you?')

But assuming that you're not Messi, your team will be much more **successful** if you pass the ball to other players every now and again.

Practise passing in pairs. Lay out two pairs of cones like small goals, and each of you stands behind your 'goal' line. Kick the ball between you, making sure it goes through the cones each time.

Try moving the 'goals' further apart, so you have to kick the ball **harder** and more **accurately.** Eventually you can have them so far away that you are in completely different villages!

163

In **Inter-dimensional Football** we practise kicking the ball between **planets.** The problem is that it takes so long to get the ball from one planet to another that by the time your pass has arrived, your teammate has got bored, gone home for their tea, eaten their tea, gone to bed, woken up the next morning, gone to school, come home again, had some more tea, done this repeatedly thousands of times, grown up into an adult, got a job, stopped playing football and isn't wearing the right boots when the ball eventually lands at their feet. In my opinion it's a bad use of time and space but we do it anyway, even though our coach says it's a **waste of balls.**

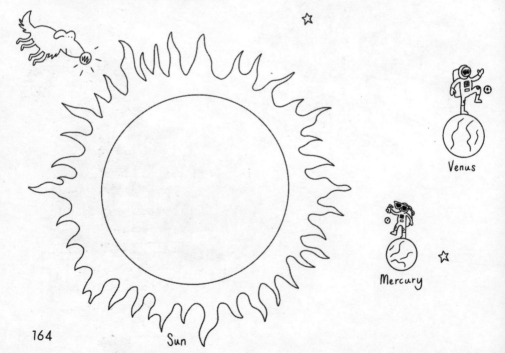

Venus

Mercury

Sun

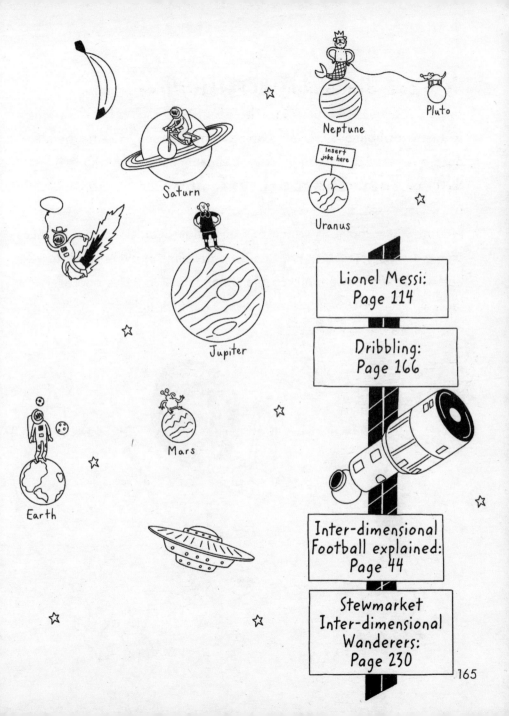

Pluto

Neptune

Insert joke here

Uranus

Saturn

Jupiter

Mars

Earth

Lionel Messi:
Page 114

Dribbling:
Page 166

Inter-dimensional
Football explained:
Page 44

Stewmarket
Inter-dimensional
Wanderers:
Page 230

Dribbling

Mostly, dribbling is about running with the ball. When it gets harder, of course, is when your opponents do everything they can to try and **get the ball off you.**

(You may also have to watch out for golden retrievers, polar bears and giant **man-eating** snails, depending on where you live – but mainly it's just people on the other team.)

You can improve your chances of dribbling past a defender by making them think you're going one way when you're actually going another. This can include spinning around, stepping over the ball, randomly yelling words like **'Bumpackets!'** and **'Fridgewater!'** and doing **jinxy things** with your feet.

My son, Hayden, does the strangest thing when he is dribbling. He sort of wobbles from side to side whilst talking to himself. He does this with his head down, and never looks up to see where he is going. Once he accidentally **dribble-wobbled** out of the back gate and down the road. He was halfway to the next village before he realised what was going on.

League table of picnic ruinations: Page 222

Tackling: Page 172

Footballer positions: Page 151

Signature moves: Page 63

Bumpackets

167

Tiny ball training drills

If you want to get really good at football, practise **all of these skills** with a tennis ball, which, of course, is a lot smaller. Try kicking the ball at a wall, controlling it, kicking it back again. The great thing about this is that you don't need anyone else to play with.

Can I play with you?

I'd love to. Well, secretly I would love to go on adventures, explore the world and fall in love with street furniture but I can't cos I'm holding the roof up.

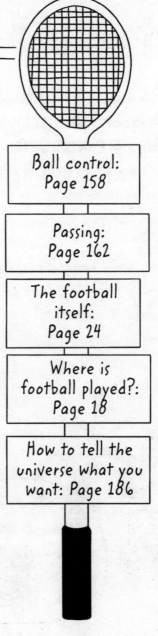

With a tennis ball, you have to hit the ball exactly in the right place. At first it will go in the wrong direction and you'll spend a lot of time chasing it. But eventually, you'll learn to control this tiny ball with your foot.

Then, when you play with a real football it will be so easy to kick it right. It'll look like the biggest target ever.

Ball control:
Page 158

Passing:
Page 162

The football itself:
Page 24

Where is football played?:
Page 18

How to tell the universe what you want: Page 186

Penalties

If someone does a **foul** close to the goal, the other team may get to take a **penalty shot** at the other team's goal. It's good to **practise** these. If you've got someone to play with – a friend, a brother, a sister, a strange uncle who has recently returned from being stranded on a desert island – then penalties are lots of fun.

Take turns being penalty-taker and goalkeeper. Do five each and see who has scored the most goals. If it's a tie then you go to **sudden death!**

Which is more scary than it sounds!

And quite complicated to explain.

You carry on taking it in turns and ...

... if the first player scores and the second player doesn't then the first player wins, **but** if the first player scores and the second player also scores then the first player goes again, **but** if the first player misses and the second player scores then the second player wins, **but** if the first player misses and the second player misses then you start again with the first player ...

So basically, during each round if someone does better than the other they win. And if it's still equal they start again.

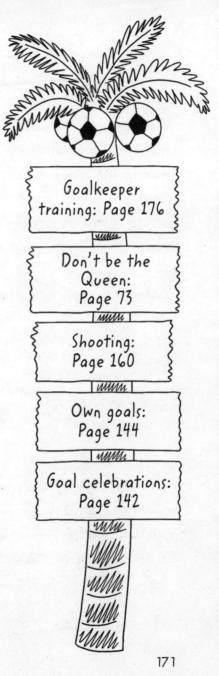

Goalkeeper training: Page 176

Don't be the Queen: Page 73

Shooting: Page 160

Own goals: Page 144

Goal celebrations: Page 142

Tackling

Trying to get the ball off an opponent is called tackling. You can tackle your own teammate if you want to **but** it's a bit pointless and you will look very silly.

When I was at school I was always afraid of tackling anyone in case I hurt myself, hurt them or hurt the ball.

Footballs do get hurt sometimes.

Charity for damaged footballs: Page 204

The beginning of my footballing career: Page 30

So what I usually did was go in **bum-first** like I was heading for a giant, invisible toilet. I'd try to use my bottom to push the other player out of the way. It very rarely worked and I did get some serious **bum injuries.**

When tackling, it's very easy to accidentally stand on someone's foot, kick someone in the shin or boot them in the bottom. In an actual match, all of those things are a **foul** and might get you sent off so you must learn not to do them!

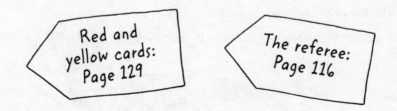

Red and yellow cards: Page 129

The referee: Page 116

Marking

Defenders often do a thing called marking, which is when you stay close to a particular striker.

Footballer positions: Page 151

Marking has nothing to do with **marker pens.** You are **not allowed** to carry a pen on the pitch with you. You are not allowed to draw pretend **tattoos** on your arms while you're supposed to be concentrating on the game. You are not allowed to write **rude words** on the back of your opponent's neck. That is a foul and you will get a yellow card. You are also not allowed to write, **'The referee has a face like a jelly'** on the yellow card. If you do that, you will get a red card and a grown-up will take the marker pen away and put it in a special drawer that you can't reach. Just leave the marker pen at home!

The referee has a face like jelly

If you're given a player to mark, your job is to make their game as hard as possible. Try and intercept any passes to them. Get between them and your goal to make it hard for them to score. Tackle them when they have the ball. At all times you should be thinking:

1. Where is the person I'm marking?

2. Where is my goal?

3. When is it half-time because I really need a poo?

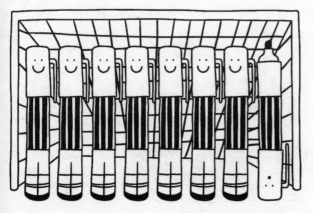

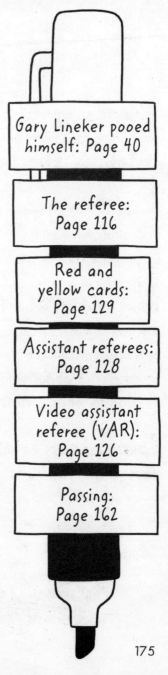

Gary Lineker pooed himself: Page 40

The referee: Page 116

Red and yellow cards: Page 129

Assistant referees: Page 128

Video assistant referee (VAR): Page 126

Passing: Page 162

Goalkeeper training

If you're going to be a keeper you need to work on your strength and agility, but mainly you need to spend a lot of time **catching the ball.**

If you've got someone to practise with, get them to take shots at you all day long. If you're on your own, spend a couple of hours kicking the ball at the wall and stopping it with your hands.

You could get your **granny** or **grandpa** to throw the ball towards you so you can practise catching it. Most grandparents will do this all day. They might, however, also tell you weird stories about what you were like as a baby or leave halfway through to make a **moussaka.**

And according to some, when you're in goal, singing **pop songs** really helps you concentrate.

Don't be the Queen: Page 73

Handball: Page 130

Lev Yashin: Page 86

Hope Solo: Page 69

Free kicks

Direct free kicks are very **exciting** because they often lead to a goal. The defending team will organise their players into a **wall** between you and the goal. If you want to score, you'll need to shoot over or around the wall.

You can practise at home by positioning cones, garden furniture or sleeping grandparents on sun-loungers to represent goal posts, goalkeepers and walls of defenders. Then all you need to do is try some of these special shots ...

Why grown-ups rest their eyes: The Funny Life of Sharks: Page 166

Different ways of playing football: Page 36

Zico: Page 72

Goalkeeper training: Page 176

Free kicks here

BENDING SHOT

To **bend** the ball around the wall you have to hit it slightly sideways, either with the inside of your boot or the outside. The inside spins it one way, the outside spins it the other.

At first, you'll send the ball in all sorts of **weird directions.** Sometimes you'll completely miss it and slip over into a pot of geraniums.

It took me a long time to learn how to bend the ball. Eventually I realised that I wasn't kicking it hard enough. When Lionel Messi takes a free kick, the ball is usually travelling at about **80 miles per hour!**

So that's what you need to learn to do. Hit it hard and perfectly. Just watch out for your grandparents!

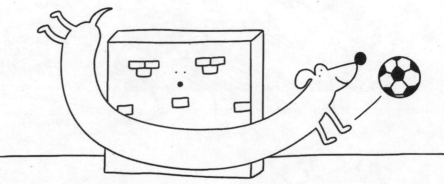

Lionel Messi:
Page 114

Inter-dimensional
Football explained:
Page 44

DIPPING SHOT

It's also possible to make the ball go up and over the wall.

Dipping shots are one of those things that I know how to do, but I just can't seem to make it happen. **It's very similar to the dishwasher.** I understand how it works. I know which buttons to press. But I always seem to get it wrong. Maybe I'm kicking the dishwasher in the wrong place.

Corners

This is when you get to put the ball by one of the corner flags and kick it in towards the goal. It's a bit like a free kick **except** the ball starts off lined up with the goal so it's very hard to score directly.

Usually, the ball gets kicked into the box and all the attackers **jump** into the air to try and head it into the goal, while the defenders do the same but try and get it away from the goal.

With so many players in a small space at the same time, funny things can happen. These include:

- Shirts being pulled

- Shorts falling down

- Boots flying off

- Faces getting elbows in them

- Secret kittens falling out of pockets

- Unscheduled Poo Situations

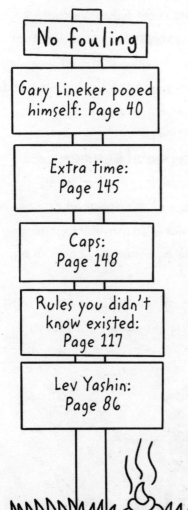

No fouling

Gary Lineker pooed himself: Page 40

Extra time: Page 145

Caps: Page 148

Rules you didn't know existed: Page 117

Lev Yashin: Page 86

If you are the goalkeeper it's your job to **organise** your defenders, **shout** a lot, **catch** any secret kittens that fall out of someone's pocket and **avoid** catching anything falling out of an Unscheduled Poo Situation.

Set pieces

Most of the time in football, you don't know what's going to happen next. **But** sometimes, your team will have the opportunity to do a **particular move** (or set piece) that you have been practising. For example, if you get a free kick you can signal to your teammates which set piece they should do and then do it.

The main idea is to **confuse the goalkeeper.** Make them wonder who is actually taking the kick and from what angle. If you want to be really cunning you can pretend to have arguments, fall over or get your teammates to run in front of you just as you're about to kick the ball. Be as creative as you want.

You can also use set pieces in everyday life. Let's say you want your parents or guardians to agree to let you watch a movie on a **school night.** You need to work with your brothers and sisters on a pre-arranged set piece ...

Below are two scripts.

SHANNON: Hi Mum.

MUM: Hi.

TYLER: We really love you.
Can we watch a film tonight?

MUMMY: No. It's a school night.

This is just **terrible**
– it's like telling everyone that
you're going to take a free kick
and pointing at the spot in the goal that you're aiming for.

It's much better to be **manipulative** and **cunning**
like this:

SHANNON: Tyler, thank you so much for helping me with my
homework today, I really appreciate it.

TYLER: That's okay.

SHANNON: Oh, I put your bike in the shed for you cos it's going to rain tonight.

TYLER: That's really thoughtful, thank you.

MUM: You two seem to be getting on very nicely this afternoon.

SHANNON: Yes, it's all thanks to that advice Mummy gave us yesterday about empathy and understanding.

MUMMY: It's nice to know someone listens to me occasionally.

TYLER: Would it be okay if we watched a film tonight?

MUM: I don't see why not.

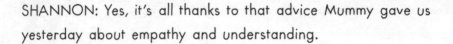

SHANNON & TYLER: **Gooooooooaaaaaaallllll!!!!!!**

In this situation, Mum is the **opposition goalkeeper** and Tyler and Shannon just played a crafty **one-two set piece** which put her off balance by making her think they weren't going to shoot when they did. Mummy is the **manager** of the team who thinks they're in charge but really has no power over what happens on the pitch at all.

GREAT PLAYERS OF ALL TIME

Famous for: Being one of the best blind footballers in the world. In Blind Football, spectators have to remain completely silent so the players can hear each other and the ball (which has a speaker playing football chants, so players can hear it coming). The game is very much about keeping control of the ball, so Blind players are often incredible at dribbling.

ABDERRAZAK HATTAB

FOOTBALLING ERA: 2010s, 2020s.

DESCRIPTION: Super-sensory Sensation.

PLAYS FOR: Morocco.

POSITION: Forward.

Bonus stuff: Blind Football can be played by anyone with a visual impairment. It became a Paralympic sport in 2004 and the International Blind Sports Association also organises a World Championship.

Para football: Page 106

Different ways of playing football: page 36

How to tell the universe what you want

I spend most of my time thinking. Usually, I am thinking the same thought **over and over** again. Even though the thought seems quite new to me, I then realise that I have actually had that thought before. I just hadn't thought of it for a while.

When I do some things, however, I stop thinking. This happens when I'm writing, playing with my children, being chased by a dog and **playing football.**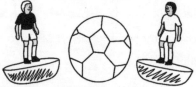

Maybe you're the same. When you're playing football, you don't worry about homework, what time dinner is, or what someone said to you at school.

You are just playing football.

When we are in that **state of flow** it feels like we are doing **exactly** the right thing in **exactly** the right way. **We are in tune with the universe.**

This is the moment to **tell the universe what you**

want. You might say some sort of prayer – perhaps to your god, or the universe, or the intergalactic mermaids. Whatever you want, let the universe know.

Every now and again, it works! And it feels **amazing.**

I think this happens more in sport because it's easy to be clear about what you're asking for.

Please can I score this goal...

Please can I save this penalty...

Please can I get through this game without pooing myself...

The rest of life, however, is **so complicated** that the intergalactic mermaids (or whoever) can't work out what it is we actually want.

So, find somewhere quiet and try telling the universe what you want to happen that day.

If you find a way that works for you, please let me know by emailing: intergalacticmermaids@seriouslykeepthisstufftoyourself.org

MIA HAMM

FOOTBALLING ERA:
1980s, 1990s, 2000s.

DESCRIPTION: A shining beacon of goal-scoring glory!

PLAYED FOR: USA.

POSITION: Midfielder / forward.

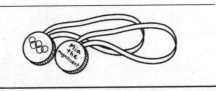

Famous for: Winning **two World Cups, scoring 158 goals** in national competitions and winning **two Olympic gold medals.** Hamm played in her first football team at the age of five. By the time she was fifteen, she was playing for the USA.

Throughout her career, Hamm has also featured in TV commercials and endorsed the first Soccer Barbie Doll. I'm looking forward to the day that someone asks me to endorse an Author Barbie Doll. But I'm not sure how successful the doll would be if it just sat around all day in its pyjamas mumbling to itself.

The manager

You can't just have eleven people running around being a football team with no one **in charge.** Someone needs to lead them and shout instructions.

The manager has many jobs which include **picking** the team, **deciding** on the tactics and then **changing things** in the middle of a match if they need changing. Managers also need to be able to use the **Hairdryer Treatment** which is one of the two following things:

1. After the match, the players have a shower and then the manager dries their hair for them, listens to their problems and suggests a better shampoo than the one they're using.

Or:

2. After the match, the manager shouts and screams at the players from very close up and sounds a bit like a hairdryer.

If that sounds like your sort of thing maybe you should become a football manager. You will need to know the following ...

Formations

Ask another football fan what they think about formations and you will soon find yourselves saying random numbers really quickly.

All these numbers are just different ways of **arranging players** on the pitch. They don't have to stay in these positions all the time, but it's helpful if everyone knows roughly where they are supposed to be and where everyone else is.

Here are some diagrams of the most popular formations:

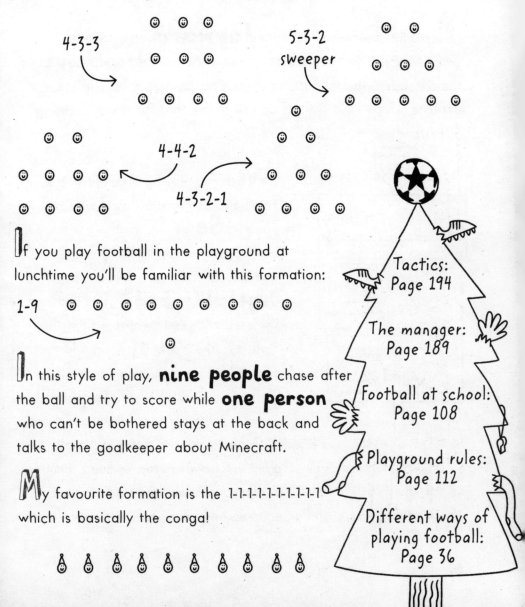

4-3-3

5-3-2 sweeper

4-4-2

4-3-2-1

If you play football in the playground at lunchtime you'll be familiar with this formation:

1-9

In this style of play, **nine people** chase after the ball and try to score while **one person** who can't be bothered stays at the back and talks to the goalkeeper about Minecraft.

My favourite formation is the 1-1-1-1-1-1-1-1-1-1 which is basically the conga!

Tactics:
Page 194

The manager:
Page 189

Football at school:
Page 108

Playground rules:
Page 112

Different ways of playing football:
Page 36

False 9

Normally, the Number 9 is a **forward** who tries to score. A False 9, **however,** stays deep and **draws out** the defender who is marking them. This creates a hole in the defence which other forwards can sneak into for handy scoring opportunities.

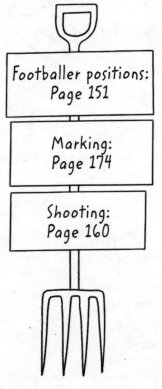

Footballer positions:
Page 151

Marking:
Page 174

Shooting:
Page 160

When I'm playing Inter-dimensional Football I like to play as a kind of False 1. **So** I look like the goalkeeper but I come out on to the pitch and do stuff. Once I dug a quick **vegetable bed** and sowed some carrot seeds whilst waiting for Yoda to take a free kick. I made the mistake of doing it on a windy day though so most of them blew away as carrot seeds are really light and small. With hindsight I should have a put a plank of wood on top to keep them in place. Just until they germinated of course. And of course, with even more

hindsight, I probably should have stayed in my goal as while I was doing this the other team scored three times.

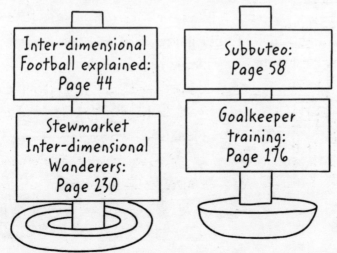

Inter-dimensional
Football explained:
Page 44

Subbuteo:
Page 58

Stewmarket
Inter-dimensional
Wanderers:
Page 230

Goalkeeper
training:
Page 176

Tactics

These are **slightly** different from formations, but some formations work better with tactics. Here are some of the main tactics you might use:

ALL-IN TACTICS

Everyone follows the ball wherever it goes on the pitch. It doesn't really work but it's lots of fun and at least everyone is involved.

THE LONG BALL

Boot it up to some big person at the front! Everyone's job is to try and **kick the ball** all the way to them, so they can score.

This is a good tactic to use if you only have one decent player. It's also helpful if that one player is really tall.

Are you sure you're in our year?

Yes. I am the same as you.

But you have a moustache. And a job at the steelworks.

TIKI-TAKA

This sounds like a type of **fish** but is actually a tactic invented by the Spanish. The idea is to keep the ball going backwards and forwards without the opposition getting it. Hopefully this will wear them out and you can take advantage when they leave holes in their defence.

Tiki-taka is probably the most entertaining football to watch, apart from maybe when footballers wear fancy dress and sing songs from Broadway shows while they play. That's definitely the most entertaining football to watch.

COUNTER-ATTACK

Everyone sits back but has to be ready to jump in and intercept a sloppy pass. Then it's all about getting the ball forward and attacking before the other team have realised what is going on.

Counter-attack has nothing to do with attacking the counter in the delicatessen.

PARK THE BUS

This is an extremely **boring** tactic to make sure you don't lose. You probably won't win either, but you can use this to try and get a draw.

The idea is to play everyone really defensively and don't even try to score. This makes it very difficult for the other team to get a goal in.

It's like parking a bus across the goal.

Make sure you don't use an actual bus. Or a blue whale. Or a wall of giraffes.

You could, however, do what Lev Yashin did and use your spider powers to build a web across the whole goal ...

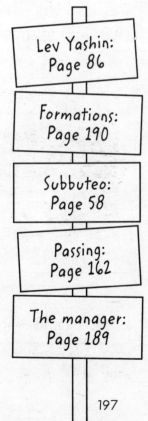

Lev Yashin:
Page 86

Formations:
Page 190

Subbuteo:
Page 58

Passing:
Page 162

The manager:
Page 189

Groundspeople

Pitches don't look after themselves. They need a **team** of people to look after them.

Wherever you play football, spare a thought for the groundspeople who give up their time to **mow, water, seed** and **repair** divots in the pitch you are playing on.

Groundspeople are also responsible for making the white lines on the pitch, which looks like lots of fun. But if you think about it, they spend most of their time either watching grass grow or watching paint dry. Both of which are some of the most **boring things in the world.**

The Most Boring Thing In The World Paradox: Page 214

Where is football played?: Page 18

Stadiums: Page 98

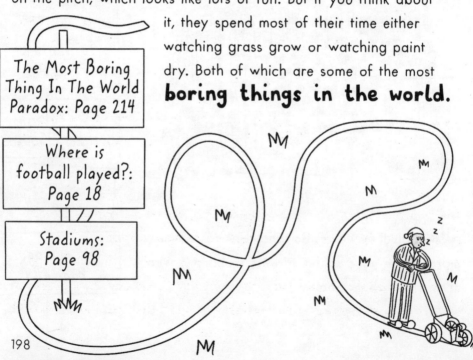

MARTA

FOOTBALLING
ERA: 2000s, 2010s, 2020s.

DESCRIPTION:
She's too speedy to tell!

PLAYS FOR: Brazil.

POSITION: Forward.

Famous for: Being the only player to have scored a goal in **five** separate World Cups. She has also been named FIFA World Player of the Year **six** times.

Marta is an incredibly fast, skilful and creative player. She has amazing control of the ball and seems to be able to dance around defenders almost as though they are nothing more than a minor irritation.

Marta is also a United Nations Goodwill Ambassador. She uses that role to promote gender equality in sports all around the world.

Mascots

For some weird reason, a long time ago, someone thought it would be a great idea for each football team to have a mascot – a person dressed up as some sort of **creature** or **animal**, usually in the team colours.

It's the mascot's job to walk around before the match and at half-time so that fans have got something to **laugh** at.

Some mascots are very **strange looking.**

Partick Thistle has a **terrifying** yellow thistle which looks more like an angry spot that has exploded.

Forest Green Rovers has a **scary-looking** cow / bull / dragon / thing. I don't think anyone is sure what it is.

The big question with mascots of course, is: **who is in the suit?** Is it an out-of-work actor? Is it really a famous person who wants to watch the match without being bothered by anyone? Is it someone being punished for committing a crime?

201

Match-fixing

Have you ever broken a matchstick? Well match-fixing will not help you in the slightest.

No, match-fixing is when criminals offer money to players or referees to fix the outcome of a match so they can place bets and **win.** This doesn't happen very often but when it does it's **big news.** People go to prison and get banned from playing, and teams get relegated to the division below.

The criminal gangs who do this are usually lunch servers at primary schools. Most of these devious robbers only work as lunch servers so they can explain to the authorities where they get their money from. Really, of course, **lunch servers** form a kind of cabbagey Mafia that needs **stamping out.**

Keep an eye on the servers at your school. If any of them offer you **extra pink sponge** to let a goal in at the next school football tournament, report them to the police immediately. Or get some friends together to form a detective gang and investigate yourselves.

Give racism the red card

There's nothing really funny to say about this page. Racism in football is when players, officials or fans are abused or treated differently because of their skin colour, religion or ethnicity. It's been a problem for far too long and is sadly still an issue today. There's no place for racism in football and everyone should be free to enjoy the game without fear or discrimination. We all need to work together to put a stop to racism, on, and off, the pitch.

You might have seen players kneeling down, or 'taking the knee', at the start of matches. This is an anti-racist gesture people use to show their support for racial equality. You don't need to be Black to take the knee before a match. In fact, it's important that everyone from all backgrounds stands up to racism. So do your bit. If you ever hear of anyone being racist to you or to anyone else, call it out or speak to a grown-up about it.

Football can be played by everyone and diversity should be celebrated. It's one of the things that makes the world such a wonderful place.

Charity for damaged footballs

We've all seen the terrible state that footballs can get into. Cheap ones that you buy at the beach get popped as soon as they even look at a **pebble.**

Even that expensive one that your uncle got you for your birthday got scuffed. The logos – once bright and clear – are now rubbed off by thousands of boots, hoofs and lobs.

Henry VIII's football

World cup 1966

eau de foot

Milk cup 1986

I think there should be a charity for damaged footballs to **repair** them and give them a happy retirement in a **nice grassy field.** Somewhere away from the fear of being kicked.

I have been talking to my friends at the Airedale Air Museum and thankfully they have donated some air to help re-inflate flat balls.

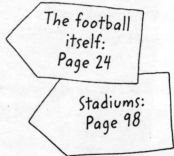

The football itself: Page 24

Stadiums: Page 98

International idioms

Different countries have different idioms, or ways of describing things that happen on the pitch. Here are some brilliant **football idioms** from around the world:

The referee is a Wellington boot (Poland) – I really like my wellies, but I'm guessing Polish people think of them as something that just stands around in the mud, not really watching anything.

Fox in the box (UK) – describes a striker who is very handy at knocking in crosses, usually by sticking out their leg and hopping.

Little flip-flop (Brazil) – a player who never seems to recover from injury so is always walking around in flip-flops.

Lettuce hands (Brazil) – a goalkeeper who misses saves.

Skied it (UK) – when you kick the ball so wildly that it flies up into the air behind the goal. In Indonesia, however, they call it *mengganggu penerbangan domestik* – a shot that 'has a high chance of disrupting a domestic aeroplane flight'.

Having square feet (France) – how you are described if your passes are terrible.

Even the ball gets in your way (Portugal) – a phrase that describes a player who is having a bad match.

The ball is round (Georgia) – fans in Georgia, as well as countries such as Norway and Germany, use this phrase to mean that anything can happen. As in:

We're 3 – 0 down with ten minutes to go.

Yes – but the ball is round.

Clear the cobwebs (France) – used to describe a player putting a shot in the top corner of the goal.

Little angel on their crossbar

(The Netherlands) – a phrase used when a keeper is saving a lot of shots.

The Finnish word **pihkatappi** means a plug that **a bear puts in its bottom when hibernating.** (Otherwise it might accidentally poo itself when asleep, and all the other bears in the cave would complain.) But anyway – in Finland, *pihkatappi* is also used to describe a defensive midfielder who **plugs the hole in between midfield and defence.** I wonder if Gary Lineker knows anything about bears. He could have done with a *pihkatappi* to stop himself from pooing his shorts during that match at Italia '90.

In the language of Yoruba (spoken in Nigeria and Benin) they use the phrase **Dundee United.** This harks back to 1972, when Scottish team Dundee United toured Nigeria. The Scots didn't prepare very well and were surprised that it was so hot. They all got sick and played terribly. Brilliantly though, the phrase **Dundee United** has survived in Yoruba. It means someone who is a **complete idiot.**

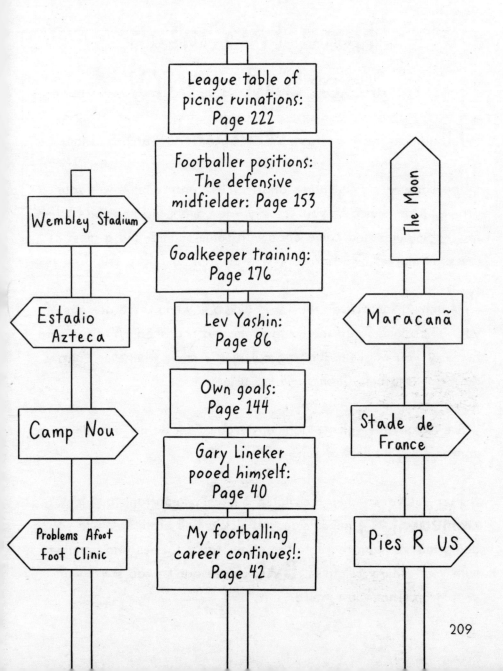

Wembley Stadium

League table of picnic ruinations: Page 222

The Moon

Footballer positions: The defensive midfielder: Page 153

Estadio Azteca

Goalkeeper training: Page 176

Maracanã

Lev Yashin: Page 86

Own goals: Page 144

Camp Nou

Stade de France

Gary Lineker pooed himself: Page 40

Problems Afoot Foot Clinic

My footballing career continues!: Page 42

Pies R US

How to watch football on TV

You don't have to go to a **stadium** to watch football.

You can just stay at home and watch it on the telly with your grown-up of choice. If you're lucky, they might nip into the kitchen for five minutes and come back with some scones and a glass of the supermarket own-brand version of your favourite drink.

Watching football on the TV is **best** when there are lots of you, all crammed into the living room and squashed on to the sofa. Some of you will keep jumping out of the chair whenever your team gets the ball. Others will fall asleep.

I like to turn the volume right down and then do my own commentary. It's lots of fun.

After you've watched the match it is very important to **immediately** go outside and kick a ball around. While you're doing this you can recreate the goals, fouls, tackles and penalties with your elderly relatives. **But** please don't swap shirts with your gran. That's just weird.

Stadiums:
Page 98

Goal
celebrations:
Page 142

Tackling:
Page 172

Penalties:
Page 170

Using football as a
way to communicate
better: Page 20

Strange things on club badges

Every football team has a badge which their players wear on the front of their tops.

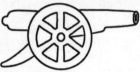

And each one is **different.**

Arsenal has a cannon on theirs. **Chelsea** has a lion who is not looking where he's going. **Barca** just has a football. **Benevento** in Italy has a witch! **The Orlando Pirates** have a skull and crossbones. My team, **Stewmarket Inter-dimensional Wanderers**, has a sugar-beet flying through space.

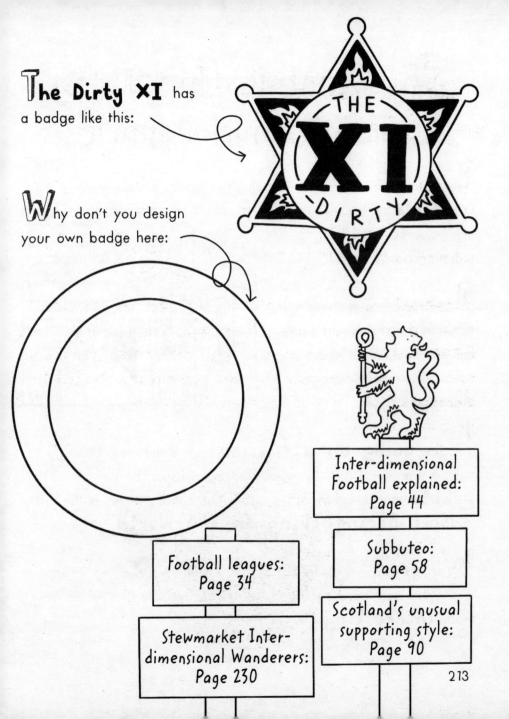

The **Dirty XI** has a badge like this:

THE
XI
DIRTY

Why don't you design your own badge here:

Inter-dimensional Football explained:
Page 44

Football leagues:
Page 34

Subbuteo:
Page 58

Stewmarket Inter-dimensional Wanderers:
Page 230

Scotland's unusual supporting style:
Page 90

The Most Boring Thing In The World Paradox

Be careful of saying that something is the most boring thing in the world because you might be falling into a **paradox trap.**

This is the most boring thing in the world.

A paradox is something that **sounds** like it makes sense, but when you think about it you realise that it is actually impossible.

Imagine **going on a mission** to find the most boring thing in the world. Let's say you find a particular kind of **pebble,** and everyone agrees that this pebble deserves the title of **Most Boring Thing In The World.**

Well, now you've given it that title, I really want to see it. I want to see the most boring thing in the world. Because that would be really **interesting.**

So as soon as you decide that anything is the most boring thing in the world, it becomes really interesting. Which means that it **can't** be the most boring thing in the world. It's actually the **second** most boring thing that is the most boring thing. **But** because that's now become the most boring thing in the world, it **isn't the most boring either.** It's the **third** most boring thing. And so on.

Until eventually you realise that there is **no** most boring thing in the world.

So don't **ever** say that anything is the most boring thing in the world, whether it's a maths lesson, a pebble, a story your little sister is trying to tell you or a football team's 7-2-1 formation.

This is the most boring thing I've ever read.

Who plays football?: Page 14

Formations: Page 190

Groundspeople: Page 198

The Great Stamford Meadows Match

My mum's mum – who we called Nanny – died in 2017. She had been very poorly for a long time and the whole family put a lot of time, effort and **love** into looking after her.

After Nanny died, her five children lost a common purpose and didn't really know what to do. A year later, we held a **big family get-together** in a little town called Stamford. We had a big lunch and then went off to the meadows to enjoy the sunshine.

But everyone felt sad and there were arguments between particular people. I don't think any of us really knew how to talk about the grief we were all experiencing.

Fortunately, Hayden had brought a football with him.

Nobody really wanted to play football. But I insisted.

Jumpers became goalposts. Teams were formed. Rules were discussed and then ignored. Not everyone played. Some sat and watched, and then stopped watching and talked. But those who played, played the **best** match of their lives.

Afterwards, everyone agreed that a **family football match** had been exactly what was needed. I suppose we all managed to communicate without really talking.

Sometimes it can be really hard to know what to do next.

When you can't think of anything else, though, kicking a ball around for an hour or so with people you love can be **exactly the right thing to do.**

Using football as a way to communicate better: Page 20

Different ways of playing football: Page 36

My footballing career continues!: Page 42

How to tell the universe what you want: Page 186

Other football positions named after household items

The defensive position of 'sweeper' (made popular by Beckenbauer) is so called because the player sweeps up any balls or attackers that make it through the defensive line.

But what other positions or things in football are named after household objects?

THE BLENDER – a midfielder who stands around in the middle of the pitch, spinning about and making a lot of noise but without actually doing anything useful.

THE SIDEBOARD – a defender who is so square and solid that the opposition finds it hard to get round them. During free kicks they pretty much make a wall by themselves.

THE PASTA MACHINE – a player who cost a lot of money but never gets used. They just sit on the subs bench gathering dust.

THE DVD PLAYER – an old player. No one is quite sure why they are kept around because they are pretty much obsolete now.

THE DISHWASHER – an enigmatic player that no one understands. They have genius in there somewhere. They do amazing things but no one has any idea how they actually work.

THE LAWNMOWER – spends a lot of time face down on the grass.

> Franz Beckenbauer: Page 150

> Corners: Page 180

> Johan Cruyff: Page 156

> Footballer positions: Page 151

☆ Your favourite ☆ player

In this book I have included profiles of lots of players that I think are some of the **greatest** in the world. It's not meant to include ALL of them because then the book would be **too long** and it would be so **heavy** you wouldn't be able to pick it up!

So I probably haven't included **your** favourite footballer. Your footballer might be someone I have never heard of. It might be someone who plays for your local team. Or your sister. Or your mum, dad or other grown-up. It might even be your pet rabbit.

On the page opposite please fill in your own Great Player of All Time Profile.

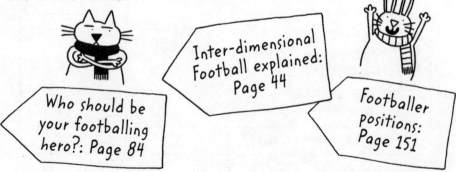

Who should be your footballing hero?: Page 84

Inter-dimensional Football explained: Page 44

Footballer positions: Page 151

GREAT PLAYER OF ALL TIME

NAME:
_____

FOOTBALLING ERA:
_____

DESCRIPTION:
_____

_____

PLAYED FOR:
_____

_____

POSITION:
_____

RANDOM FACT:
_____

_____

BRILLIANT STAT:
_____

_____

League table of picnic ruinations

Having a picnic **always** sounds like a nice idea. I love picnics. Food eaten outside always tastes better. Or, in the case of my mum's homemade sausage rolls, slightly less awful.

Some people **hate** picnics. They say it's just lunch with nowhere to sit. They say only mad people have picnics and it should be **illegal.**

What's for sure, however, is that a perfectly good picnic can be ruined by the following list of things:

CHOCOLATE:

It sounds delicious, but when it's hot and sunny chocolate melts and coats the inside of everything with itself. **Sticky nightmare!**

SOMEONE ELSE'S GOLDEN RETRIEVER:

Literally the most **enthusiastic** animal in the world. Will bound on to your blanket and eat your pork pie. 'It was on the floor so I assumed it was mine,' the big yellow flopperwapper says as it pants off again with a face full of booty.

FOOTBALL:

Imagine you're having a picnic so you can propose marriage. You're about to pop the question when a wet football hits your beloved **in the face.**

Ball control: Page 158

GETTING LOST:

WASPS:

These little **bumpackets** can smell a picnic from a mile away. They are particularly good at landing on the jam smeared on a small child's face. Picnic - **RUINED.**

BEARS:

RAIN:

Whatever the weather forecast says, if you're having a picnic you'd better take a **massive umbrella**, some **waterproof clothes** and at least **ten pairs of welly boots.** Rain doesn't care if it's been forecasted or not.

HURRICANE:

You will not be able to hold on to your picnic blanket or the people you came with if a **hurricane** turns up at your picnic. Tie yourself to a tree and put a Scotch egg between your teeth to stop yourself from screaming.

Scotland's unusual supporting style: Page 90

MANKY BLANKET:

Football fan quiz

If you've got this far into the book then, **congratulations!**

I bet you think you're a bit of a **football expert** now.

Well, why not try this quiz and see how you get on.

Answers are **not** at the back of the book. There aren't enough pages.

1. The ancient Japanese version of Keepy-uppy is called:

a) Kemari

b) Kawasaki

c) Kalahari

2. Eusébio was born in Mozambique, but which European country did he play for?

a) Portugal

b) Pootugal

c) Portupoo

3. Franz Beckenbauer pretty much invented which position?

a Sweeper

b) Hoover

c) Bribe-collector

4. Brazilian player Marta holds which world renowned position?

a) United Nations Goodwill Ambassador

b) United Nations Goodwill Flambassador

c) United Nations Goodwill Haberdasherer

5. Diego Maradona was known as what?

a) God
b) Obi Wan Kenobi
c) The Intergalactic Mermaid

6. The final of the Bopping Dogs On The Head With Sausages World Tournament is held at Wembley Stadium. But on which date?

a) 31 June
b) 30 February
c) 32 October

7. Which is the biggest stadium in Rio de Janeiro?

a) Macaranã
b) Macaroona
c) Jammidoggia

8. In England's first game in Italia '90, Gary Lineker famously did what?

a) Pooed himself
b) Did a wee on the goalpost
c) Vomited on the referee

9. The Dirty XI is one of my imaginary Inter-dimensional Football teams. But who plays in the left-back position?

a) The Big Bad Wolf
b) Dr No
c) Al from Al's Toybarn in *Toy Story* 2.

10. Why are globe artichokes a good choice for the vegetable garden?

a) They are perennials and don't need replanting each year
b) Their large leaves shade out weeds that might compete
c) They provide flowers for insects
d) All of the above.

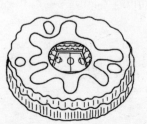

Stewmarket Inter-dimensional Wanderers

I've mentioned my team quite a lot in this book. The line-up does vary but here is our most common **Starting XI:**

I'm going for a 1-4-4-2 sweeper formation.

Why are people still using Roman numerals?: Page 70

I think **Gandalf's** magical powers and ability to see the big picture would be very helpful as a kind of midfield wizard. I have put **myself** on the wing for this team as I'm very good at running up and down and avoiding the ball. I've made **Cruyff** the captain because ... he is Cruyff. Auntie Lisa would control the midfield and Hope Solo would shut out any shots at our goal. I know that **C3PO** probably isn't the best winger, but it would be funny watching him waddle up and down the pitch complaining about everything.

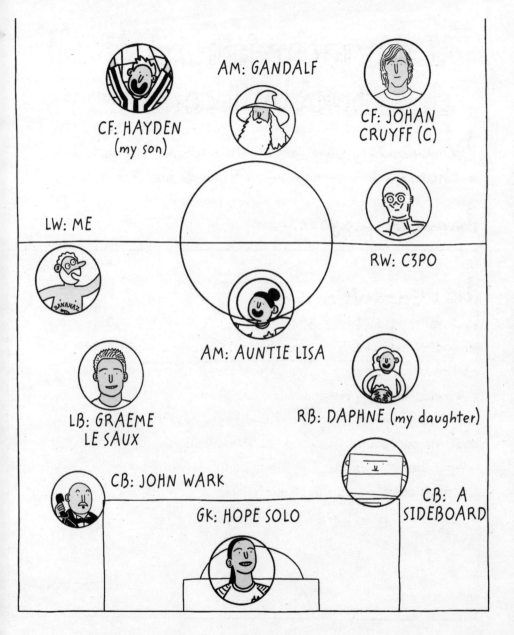

CF: HAYDEN (my son)

AM: GANDALF

CF: JOHAN CRUYFF (C)

LW: ME

RW: C3PO

AM: AUNTIE LISA

LB: GRAEME LE SAUX

RB: DAPHNE (my daughter)

CB: JOHN WARK

CB: A SIDEBOARD

GK: HOPE SOLO

Your inter-dimensional football team

What would your team look like? This template allows you to **choose** a formation as well. Just decide how they're going to play and then choose eleven blanks to fill in with your **favourite players.**

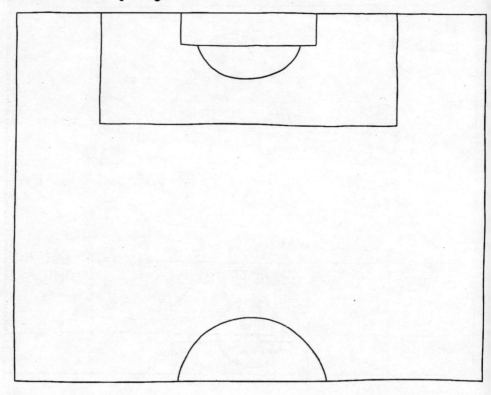

Remember they don't have to all be playing now. Some could be incredibly old. And they don't have to be professional footballers. Some could be members of your family, your friends or even fictional characters from books and films.

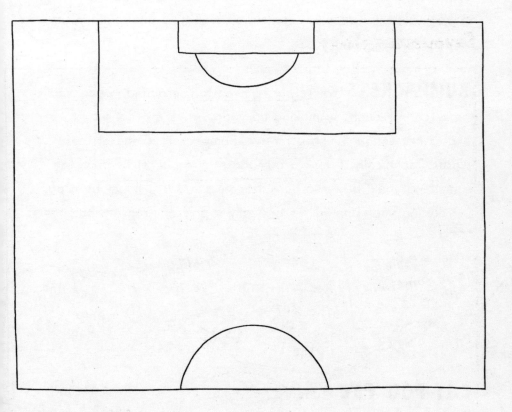

Glossary

There might have been some words in this book that you didn't understand. This is a good thing. How else are you going to learn new words? There are no limits to your reading!

Here you will find a few definitions that may not appear in a dictionary.

BUMPACKETS You're not allowed to use actual swear words on a football pitch, so making up your own is a great way to be expressive without being offensive. Bumpackets is one of these words. Technically, I think a bumpacket is a packet of bum, like something you'd buy in a bum delicatessen. Or it might be a packet for putting your bum in. So basically a pair of grease-proof pants.

League table of picnic ruinations: Page 222

Who plays football?: Page 14

Dribbling: Page 166

Red and yellow cards: Page 129

CAT-POO PIE Standard half-time food that you might eat at a football match.

Football match food: Page 111

FIFA The world governing body of football. Confusingly, it's actually French and stands for Football Internationale Falafel Abracadabra, or something.

FOOTBALL ASSOCIATION
The English governing body for football.

GENDER EQUALITY The concept
that whether you identify as male, female or non-binary, you should have equal access to sports, earning money, jobs and everything in between.

GOAL This can mean one of two things.
The Goal is the white rectangular thing at the end of the pitch. A goal is when you kick the ball into the white rectangular thing at the end of the pitch and score a point.

The FIFA World Cup: Page 136

The beginning of the FA: Page 28

Hope Solo: Page 69

Own goals: Page 144

Goal celebrations: Page 142

Shooting: Page 160

LGBTQ+ RIGHTS The concept that however a person identifies, or whoever a person loves or fancies, they should not be discriminated against or treated badly. They should have equal access to sports, earning money, jobs and everything else, too.

OLYMPIC GAMES A big sporting event that happens every four years. It's started in ancient Greece when someone accidentally ran 26 miles and ate a chocolate bar.

Football at the Olympics: Page 138

PARA SPORTS Sports played by people with a disability, including physical and intellectual disabilities. Making sure these people can participate in something they love and can train for and get into and be AMAZING at.

PENALTY This is when one of your players (possibly you) will get to put the ball on the penalty spot and try and score a goal. It's just you against the goalkeeper.

PITCH Big green rectangular thing. You can't miss it.

POSITION This is where a player usually plays. Positions are different according to what formation you are playing in.

RACISM When a single person or community discriminate against someone or treat someone badly because of the colour of their skin, religious beliefs or their ethnic group.

Where is football played?: Page 18

Footballer positions: Page 151

REFEREE The person in charge of the match. It is their job to keep everyone in line. It's your job to remember not to ignore them. Also, remember that they are not a player. There's no point passing the ball to the referee.

STADIUM Really big building with a football pitch in the middle of it. It has steps and seats and everything.

Stadiums: Page 98

TUNNEL This is the corridor from the dressing rooms to the pitch. It's here that you stand and get nervous before you're about to play.

Rules you didn't know existed: Page 117

Penalties: Page 170

Stats of the book

Football is **full** of statistics. So here are some of the stats of this book.

It was written between March and August 2020, mainly using a Lenovo ThinkPad laptop which I bought **second-hand** for £200.

Ninety-eight per cent of the book was written sitting at our kitchen table in Suffolk. Two per cent was written at my mum's house in Devon.

It contains 28,265 words.

I did a final edit of the book in my off-grid caravan, powered entirely by the Sun.

Footballers' stats include how many times players have played, how many goals they scored and how many goals they assisted. My book stats include how many times a word has appeared in the book, how many times it has appeared in the funny part, and how many times it helped set up the funny part. Here are the **top ten** performing words.

Name	Appearances	Funnies	Assists
Lineker	19	16	3
Poo	20	19	1
Ball	172	89	83
Pants	11	10	1
Weird	5	4	1
Messi	21	11	10
Ronaldo	10	2	8
Goal	146	13	16
Toilet	5	4	1
Love	11	3	5

The end page

This is the last page of the book. Congratulations on getting here. Your reward is that you get to see this picture of a naked football!

Why not go back to the beginning and start again? You might have missed something **really unimportant.** Think of yourself as a human VAR! Rewind and see if any of the words in this book are offside! If you find any please email me on the following address:

ireallyhavehadenoughnow@stoplickingdoorhandles.net

THE END